GETTING THERE & STAYING THERE

THE PEOPLE SIDE OF SUSTAINED OPERATIONAL EXCELLENCE

GREG GRAY

Carolyn,
Thanks!

3/8/17

This book is dedicated to the hundreds of people I've met over the years who pulled me aside during the breaks at my seminars and at conferences and started a whispered chat with:
"Pssst... Hey Greg! Let me tell you what's *really* going on around here!"

TABLE OF CONTENTS

INTRODUCTION

Inevitably the question will be asked, "For whom is this book intended?"

The answer is pretty straightforward: Anyone who has the task of or responsibility for getting a group of people to perform at a high level, consistently and over the long term.

This includes, but is not limited to:

- Executives, managers and supervisors
- Business Owners
- Coaches
- Band Conductors and Choir Directors
- Professors and Teachers
- Parents
- Faith leaders of congregations of any type
- Leaders of civic organizations and non-profits
- Leaders of any volunteer based organizations
- Leaders of neighborhood associations
- Leaders of booster club type organizations

Well, you get the point.

If you've ever served in one of these types of roles, you understand the challenge associated with keeping everyone on the same track, focused on the same goals, and doing all this while sustaining operational excellence in the organization.

You probably also know that no matter how sophisticated the systems, processes, and technology your organization employs, ultimately the real success of an organization lies with the people on the team.

The more engaged, focused, prepared, and motivated the people on the team are the more successful your organization will be. Conversely, if your people aren't on board with what the organization is trying to do, all the sophisticated systems, processes, and technology won't get you where you are trying to go.

My belief that this is so comes after nearly 2 decades of delivering seminars, workshops, and keynote addresses literally all over the world. Over this period of time, I've found that the most interesting things I learn about any organization and the struggles it faces are learned during the *breaks* at seminars and conferences.

Without fail, someone will come up to me and say something like:

"Pssst... Greg! Let me tell you what's *really* going on around here!"

And then we have to go out into the hallway, behind the projection screen, into a stairwell, or some other out of the way place where they can give me the *"real scoop"*.

After sharing this insider information with me, the conversation usually ends with the person saying something like this to me:

"Now this is just between me and you, right? Don't tell anyone I told you that!"

In other words, they are swearing me to secrecy.

What they share never has anything to do with proprietary information about the company or industry.

In the hundreds of these conversations that I've experienced, the common theme to them all is that there is a people component that the organization, or more specifically some of the organization's leaders, struggle to get a handle on.

That simple realization is echoed in every type of business or organization. Whether they are private enterprise or government entity, for profit or not for profit, employee based or volunteer based. And in every discipline imaginable from education to manufacturing, retail to law, travel related industries to all manner of financial institutions, religious organizations and yes, even to families.

These many conversations and my own personal experience as a manager, supervisor, and business owner combined to serve as the genesis of this book.

Reality check time: This book will not answer every question for every possible scenario. No legitimate or ethical author can or should make that claim. Instead, what we'll explore here are those challenges that are common to leaders of all stripes. And we'll deliver some solutions that most anyone can implement to make the task of effectively leading others easier, less stressful, more successful, and more satisfying.

On the concept of leadership being a gift...

I do acknowledge that effective leadership is a gift, but I believe further that most effective leaders are really just incredibly perceptive people who learn from the great examples of effective leaders they've witnessed or experienced. At the same time, they also learn from the poor examples of others. Simply put, they pay attention to what works and what doesn't and then put together the sum total of what they've learned into practice.

Finally, I should probably apologize in advance as I confess to having anything *but* Pulitzer Prize level writing skills. And in the spirit of full disclosure, I also openly admit that, as many who've attend my presentations will attest to, I am a story teller by nature, and so you can expect that trend to continue throughout this book.

I find that my understanding of things is greatly enhanced by having those lessons nested in real world situations - sometimes painful, often times funny, always real.

So that's how we'll be keeping it here - real.

CHAPTER 1

PATHETICA

I should start out by reiterating that much of the motivation for this book is driven by my personal reflections on my own first experience as a manager - specifically, the first year or so.

It's an era of my life that I look back on and refer to fondly now as "Pathetica".

That's because, quite frankly, I wasn't very good at it.

It's not that I didn't want to be good manager. I actually had every intention of being the best manager possible. I just didn't have the tools I really needed to be effective and as a result I made a lot of mistakes.

My ascension into my first role as supervisor holds some clues as to why I got off to such a rocky start. You may find that some of what I'm about to describe might sound familiar to you.

I was a customer service representative in a call center, and, If I must say so myself (and I often did), I was very good at it.

I received a lot of recognition for being a great customer service representative (CSR), and I had lots of CPS (cheap plastic stuff) awarded to me to show for it.

Our company was successful and began to grow quite rapidly and as a result, our customer base grew quickly.

With a quickly growing customer base came a need for more CSRs to handle the increase in call volume. With an increase in CSRs we quickly realized that we would need more customer service supervisors because the span of control for supervisors (the supervisor to CSR ratio) was becoming unmanageable.

Thus began my first significant journey into leadership/management. The era of "Pathetica" was about to begin.

I was approached by a number of managers with the prospect of becoming a supervisor and in most of these conversations there was great emphasis on how well I'd done the job of CSR. There were frequent expressions of my being able to lead a team with similar levels of performance as I had experienced. Even in the formal interviews for the supervisory position that followed, there was little discussion of my management skills (or lack thereof) and lots of discussion around my reputation as a great CSR.

What I'm describing to you is the prototypical conception of a micromanager.

Given the way I was approached about the job of supervisor and the subsequent interviews I went through, it was clear to me (or at least it seemed so) that what they wanted me to do was to create a team of CSRs who mirrored me as a CSR.

In other words, my take on things was that they wanted me to have my team to do things the way I'd done things as a CSR.

And just like that, a micromanager was born.

With this newfound, albeit flawed, perspective on leadership I remember my first meeting with my new team. It went something like this:

"I'm excited about being your supervisor, and while I know you have a good many ideas on how to deliver great customer service, here's how we're going to do it, because this is how I got where I am today!"

At that point, I methodically began the process of trying to turn every member of my team in to me. I told them how I spoke to customers, the words I chose to use in different scenarios, the way I noted customer accounts, how I handled complaints, etc.

Well, suffice it to say that didn't go over to well, because I had in essence begun a campaign to squash their creativity and suppress any semblance of individuality on the team.

Again, let me be clear that this wasn't my intention. I just wanted to do what I believed I was hired to do based on all the conversations and interviews I'd gone through to get the job.

As Pathetica continued, I ran into some other interesting situations.

Most notable was the fact that within 3 months of taking the helm of this particular team, the time had come for their annual merit performance reviews. You know... the "money" review.

The only problem is that I'd never given an annual merit review (or any other type of review for that matter) in my entire life, and now I was faced with the task of affecting the pay of 12 people using a tool that I had no familiarity with.

Compound this with the fact that in their employee files (they'd all been employees for a year or more), there was little or no documentation. Even the attendance records were sketchy at best.

This means I was going to be delivering annual (12 month) reviews that would actually be based on the 3 months I'd spent with them so far.

I was terrified! My only hope was that they wouldn't be able to think back past 3 months given that's all I had to go on.

Mind you, I was no wiz at documenting performance myself, given that I'd not been taught to do this either.

I can clearly recall one of those first reviews going something like this:

Me: "You're doing a good job, but I'd like to see you take more initiative in self development. Maybe a class on word processing, or something like that" (one of the performance sections in the review template was initiative in self development)

Employee: "But I took a couple of classes like that 8 months ago"

Me: "You see, that's one of your problems, you can't stay focused on what I'm talking about!"

Oops! I couldn't defend my assertion/recommendation because I didn't have the necessary historical employee data, but rather than just acknowledging that, I went into self-defense mode to "manage" the situation.

As you might imagine, word of this experience spread pretty quickly, including to HR (by the way, I hated HR when I was in Pathetica for reasons that will become clear later, if they aren't clear already).

As a result each of the other merit reviews I delivered to the other members of the team had a much more contentious feel to them because I was bracing myself for more conflict... and so were my employees.

Again, it was not my intention to be a jerk as a supervisor. But the net result was that's exactly how many of my employees perceived me, and for good reason.

And so it went for nearly a year. The turning point for me was the first supervisory skills class I attended. I got my opportunity to attend this class about 13 months *after* being promoted to supervisor.

I remember sitting in that class in abject horror as I heard all the things I should be certain not to do as a supervisor, realizing that I'd done most of those things multiple times. The thought actually crossed my mind that I'd been sent to this class so I'd know why they were going to fire me the next day.

Fortunately for me, I didn't get fired the next day, but I did realize how unprepared I was when I was initially given the job and privilege of leading others 13 months earlier.

My story, as I hear from many people, is not unlike their own story:

- Great sales people being promoted to sales managers
- Great players being hired as coaches
- Great volunteers being elected president of the organization
- Great customer service representatives being promoted to customer service supervisor
- Great contractors being promoted to project managers
- Great doctors being promoted to hospital administrators
- Great teachers being promoted to principals
- Great college professors being promoted to department chairs, deans, provosts, etc.
- Great plant workers being promoted to foremen or plant managers

And on and on it goes.

Let me be clear, great performers are not by definition poor leaders, but leadership is about much more than simply how well the leader did "the job". In fact, some of the best leaders were not known to be stellar performers or for that matter even very proficient at all in the particular discipline or skill they found themselves leading.

Great leaders do, however, consistently use techniques and skills that aid them in effectively leading others.

The truth is that many of us have experienced our own personal version of Pathetica at some point in time in our lives. But I'm proof that while you may have resided there at some point, you aren't destined to live there forever.

CHAPTER 2

LEADERSHIP REALITY CHECKS

One of the more perplexing parts of being a newly minted manager was that I discovered quite early on that just because I wanted the people on my team to do something, that didn't automatically translate into them delivering the desired behavior.

This was a sobering realization for me in that, as naive as that made me, I don't think that I ever really considered that this would be the case.

It was, however a source of considerable frustration for me, and if you've ever been in that situation, I'm certain that you'll be able to relate.

What I was missing was a series of Reality Checks that I had, to that point, not considered.

These were the kinds of things that people shared with me behind the screens, in the parking lots and in other out of the way spots during the breaks at my seminars. They were the things that reportedly some leaders don't "get", or that they used to get and have just lost touch with over time.

We'll call these things Leadership Reality Checks and believe it or not, there are 13 of them.

During Pathetica, I was aware of 5 or 6 of these Reality Checks, but not 13 of them. In retrospect, that really kind of explains some of my frustration during Pathetica.

You see, if I considered that there were 5 or 6 realities that could be derailing my ability to effectively lead my team, then it makes sense that I also had devised 5 or 6 strategies to deal with those realities. But if there were 13 "Reality Checks" (meaning that there were 7 or 8 that I hadn't considered) that means I was likely applying the wrong strategies to the realities I hadn't yet embraced.

What does that look like in the real world?

Here is a scenario that used to play out for me quite often during Pathetica.

I'd have a team of 12 people, and I'd give them all the same direction at the same time, and while 11 of the people would follow through on what I'd directed, there would always be that one person who never seemed to get it done.

This became so frustrating for me at times that I would actually bring it up in team meetings. It would go something like this:

"I asked everyone here to do the same thing. You were all here in this very room when I said it. And everyone did it... except one person. "

I would then turn to the person who failed to come through and continued, ". . . everyone did it except for you. "

And in pure Pathetica form, I went on to say, in the meeting with the whole team present, ""What is *your* problem?!"

Note: Now remember, I was operating in the heart of the Pathetica Era; meaning, it had not yet occurred to me or been brought to my attention that this probably wasn't a very good way to conduct a team meeting.

In retrospect, what I realize is that maybe the reason this person wasn't giving me the behavior that I wanted didn't exist within the 5 or 6 realities I'd considered, and therefore the strategies I was employing to gain compliant behavior were likely doomed to fail before I even put them in play.

In short, my toolbox didn't include all the tools I needed to help (or compel) this person and others to do the things I wanted or needed them to do.

In the hundreds of seminars I've done, it's not been hard to figure out that there are a lot of people that have felt the same frustration.

With that in mind, on the pages that follow we'll identify 13 Leadership Reality Checks and the requisite strategies to help us lead through them.

Let's get started.

Leadership Reality Check #1
Training doesn't always work, and there's a reason why

When a person is new to a particular role or when some aspect of that role (i. e. job responsibilities, technology, procedures, etc.) has changed, the usual prescribed remedy is to send the person to training or some type of instructional environment. In many cases this is the appropriate strategy.

That being said, here's the tricky part - sometimes people are sent to training not because they don't know *how* to do something, but rather because they are *not* doing it.

In other words, they are being sent to training because there is a *will* deficit. Not a *skill* deficit.

As someone who spent 4 years as a corporate trainer, I saw evidence of this all the time. There were people who were being sent to training not because they didn't know *how* to do something, but because they *weren't* doing it.

More recently, I did a consult with a prospective client who'd been referred to me by one of my recent clients.

The person I was consulting with was the director of a 400-person call center that provided customer service for a major cable service provider.

Here's how the conversation went:

Me: "How can I be of service?"

Them: "We need you to teach our customer service representatives how to properly greet customers who call. "

Me: "Do they not know how to properly greet callers?"

Them: "Oh no. They know how they are supposed to greet callers!"

Me: "So how do you think I might be able to help?"

Them: "We need you to get them to the point where they properly greet customers who call. "

* Awkward silence *

Me: "So they really don't know how to greet callers?"

Them: "Oh, they know exactly what they are supposed to be doing when they answer the phone!"

This back and forth went on for a few minutes. I eventually informed the prospective client that I wasn't sure that my training their employees how to answer the phones properly was going to meet their needs.

The response I got was "Listen, we hear you're good at this kind of thing, and since you have call center experience, we'd like you to do this for us".

Note: For those of you that don't know, a 24-hour call center with 400 employees who can't all be off the phones for training at the same translates into a sizeable contract for my little company.

I told the Director of the call center that, to me, it didn't seem like they were dealing with a training issue for the customer service reps. Instead, it sounded like the management team might need to spend some time investigating what was *really* going on, and that I could help them with that.

She responded that training the customer service reps was the path they wanted to take at this point.

I respectfully declined the work.

Why?

Because I knew that while I might be able to put some wind in the sails of their CSR's for a while, their behavior would likely soon revert back to where it was before and that the resulting impression would be that my company didn't deliver for the client.

Situations like this can be very problematic for any organization. If it becomes the cultural norm for individuals to be sent to training or instructional classes because of a *will* deficit vs. a *skill* deficit, a new cultural perception around training will begin to emerge. Training, which should be seen as a positive developmental and growth opportunity, will soon begin to be seen as punishment.

You'll know whether this may be happening in your organization if when you tell people they will be attending training, they respond by saying, "What did I do?!"

The point here is that training/instruction is exactly the right strategy when there is a *skill* deficit. Not when there is a *will* deficit.

Leadership Reality Check #2
Avoid Conducting "Here!" Orientation

The best example of this issue is what a person who worked for one of my clients described to me.

This person said that when you were hired or got a different job in their company, they received what he called *"Here!"* orientation for the new role. What he meant was that on the first day on the job typically what happens is that someone walks up to you with a set of files or paperwork and says *"Here!"* and then turns and walk away.

No direction. No explanation. No timelines. Just *"Here!"*

While this may be a more extreme version of what happens to some people, it is not that far out of the realm of possibility as is evidenced by the large roar of laughter that usually comes from the audience in my seminars when I share this story.

What usually happens in situations like this is that the new person, not wanting to appear uninformed (translation: stupid) or unqualified may not press the deliverer of the *"Here!"* package on what to do with it. Instead, the new person devises what tends to be a common strategy to work through this on his or her own.

What do they do? They strike out in search of others that have similar *"Here!"* packages in the hope that they'll be able to figure it out with the help of other *"Here!"* package holders. The new person usually ends up aligning himself or herself with someone who they perceive to be helpful and knowledgeable about *"Here!"* stuff.

Your hope as a leader, is that the person they align themselves with is someone who:

1. Actually does the works properly
2. Has a good attitude and approach to doing the work
3. Is not lacking in both areas.

The problem is that the new person doesn't really know who's who early on and so they could end up adopting poor work habits and a less than positive approach to the work. What's worse, you may not realize this until much later.

So how do you help them, and by extension your team when it's not clear whether or not they know what to do?

You need to make a determination as to how well clued in the person(s) in question are about your expectations for them.

Here's a starting place to see where you may be right now with how closely aligned your expectations are with those of the people on your team.

Let's say I gave you a 4x6 index card on which I asked you to write down your specific expectations for the members of your team.

Then let's say I met with each of your team members and gave them each a 4x6 index card and then asked them to write down what they thought you wrote down.

The question is "Would they write the same thing you wrote?"

If you expect that there may be any "daylight" so to speak, between what you expect and what your team members believe you expect, that will likely be problematic for your organization. It also means that there are some conversations you need to have right away.

As a word of caution, it doesn't matter how long the person has been in the role, or whether you believe they should know, or whether you think its obvious that they should know. What matters is that you make certain that the people that you lead know precisely what you expect from them.

This is, by the way, not only a good thing for you as a leader. It's a good thing for the people you lead as well.

The interesting thing about people and expectations is that they seldom operate without any. If you don't clearly communicate your expectations they will create expectations of their own, and those expectations may not be in alignment with yours. And it could take you months to find that out.

So make sure you are clearly communicating your precise expectations to those you lead and revisit the "index card test" or some version of it periodically to make sure things have not gone off track.

As an added benefit, for the more courageous leaders among you, consider asking what your people's expectations are of you. In effect, do the index card test in reverse.

In either respect, whether it's a matter of closing the gap in expectations you have for your team or vice versa, here's the real deal about the situation: If there is a gap, your people already know it and have known it for some time. They are just curious as to whether you're aware of the gap, and will be thrilled to know that you have figured it out and that you've taken steps to bridge the expectations gap - in both directions.

Leadership Reality Check #3
Because you "Said so" isn't enough

I remember, when I was back in Pathetica, that whenever I encountered a situation where I was asked the "why" question after directing someone to do something in particular, I leaned on the experience I gained from one of the early managers I had in my life.

This manager was, for the most part, a "biped" in that he walked mostly upright although he really wasn't all the way at the end of Darwinian scale of development. He did however demonstrate that he could work with tools and was familiar with fire and the wheel (enough sarcasm there for you?).

I can remember clearly asking this particular boss of mine "why" he wanted me to do something, and he responded crisply and succinctly with "Because I said so!" which is strikingly similar to what we say to our children.

Note: If you've ever thought and/or said out loud when referring to the people you lead that "These people act just like a bunch of children", consider the possibility that it may be so because that's how they are being treated or have been treated in the past.

I can even remember following the "why" question with the biped with a statement like, "Well, I was just thinking. . ." and before I could get to the end of the sentence, I was told crisply and succinctly, "I don't pay you to think."

Sadly, during Pathetica, I found myself duplicating this behavior even though in my gut, I knew it wasn't right or helpful.

Every activity in your organization should have some connection to the larger goals and objectives of your organization. Your ability to sustain optimal performance in your group is tied to how well your team understands those connections.

Here's the catch, however.

Before you can show someone the "The Big Picture", *you* have to have a clear understanding of "The Big Picture".

Further, when asked, you should be able to communicate the answer to the "why" questions (that you will at some point encounter) with precision, clarity, confidence, and ease.

If one of your team members asks you the "why" question and in answering you hesitate or stumble, you'll leave your people with one of two impressions, and likely both:

1. You don't know "why" yourself
2. You're about to make something up

If your people come to either or both of these conclusions, not only will the task or job not be handled consistently the way you want, but also your position as a leader of that group will become at that moment, compromised.

Here's an additional tip.

Let's say that you are asked "why" a particular task, procedure, or practice is being done in your organization and after thoughtful consideration you can't come up with a good answer (other than because we've always done it that way), then my advice to you is to STOP DOING THAT THING IMMEDIATELY until such time that you find a viable answer.

If you cannot find a viable answer for the "why" question, then make an unequivocal choice not to restart that activity. It is likely depleting your organization's resources without yielding meaningful results.

Leadership Reality Check #4
Everything is not of equal importance

It is not uncommon for people in your organization to have priorities that differ, conflict, or even sometimes from their perspective, outrank your priorities. I always found this incredibly frustrating to me during Pathetica because I kept coming back to the same basic thought - "I pay you, so how could you possibly believe something I want you to do is less important that what you're doing".

The fact is, however, that this can and does happen quite often in organizations. Lack of clear expectations and an understanding of "The Big Picture" are no doubt often the culprits here, but there is another layer or piece of the puzzle that can help remedy this situation.

These kinds of disconnects often signal that it's time for you to establish or reestablish priorities in your organization.

The fact is that every activity in your organization doesn't have the same weight, but unless you've clearly established and communicated organizational priorities, your team will draw their own conclusions and those conclusions as to what's most important may not be in synch with your own.

For example, getting a report completed by the end of the business day may be important, but is returning a call and resolving an issue for an irate client *more* important?

If an employee is speaking with a client who's physically in your office and the phone rings, if no one else is available to answer the phone, should that employee suspend his or her conversation with the "in person" client to answer the call? And should the phone client be informed that they'll be called back later, or should the employee handle the caller's issue at that time?

This is all about establishing priority levels in your organization.

A great metaphor is the "Big Rocks" exercise that is often used by speakers and time management trainers. I'll present a "Gregorized" version of the story here to illustrate my point

In a seminar setting, there is a 6-foot table in the front of the room.

On this table sits a large clear plastic jar, a number of big rocks about the size of your fist, a bucket containing gravel, and a bucket containing sand.

The seminar leader calls for a volunteer and informs the volunteer that his or her job is to get all of the materials on the table into the large clear plastic jar.

Then the seminar leader picks up the bucket of gravel and pours some of it into the jar saying, "You see the way I'm putting this gravel into the jar? I'd like you to get all of these items into this jar."

Often, the volunteer will proceed to put the rest of the gravel into the jar. Why? Because the volunteer takes the seminar leader's actions as a hint as to how he or she should proceed.

Mini-Lesson #1 - Your people tend to follow your lead. If you tend to handle and focus on gravel, so will they.

Now back to the story.

The volunteer quickly begins to panic a bit as they realize that the gravel has filled 3/4 of the jar and the larger rocks aren't in yet. In an effort to rectify the situation, the volunteer now proceeds to try to put the big rocks in the jar and is immediately faced with the reality that they aren't going to fit.

The volunteer then tries to place the big rocks in to the jar strategically thinking that maybe the shape of the big rocks is the key. So they arrange and rearrange the order and placement of the rocks. They try to burrow a chasm in the gravel to try to get more big rocks in. They try to force the big rocks in with brute force and are soon left with the realization that all the big rocks aren't going to fit.

So, with some of the big rocks still not in the jar, they move on to pour the sand into the jar which all fits.

When the volunteer is done, the seminar leader points out that the volunteer has made a good effort but also points out that some of the big rocks never made it into the jar.

The seminar leader then goes on to ask, "What if the big rocks represented the biggest and most important things in your life? Things like your family, your leisure time, your faith, etc.? It looks like you've chosen to include some big rocks at the expense of others. "

Mini Lesson #2: Have you ever felt this way? As if you're sacrificing some important things for others. Even in your professional life, have you found yourself or your organization choosing to act on some important objectives at the exclusion of others?

Back to the story...

Then the seminar leader lets the volunteer begin again.

As you might expect, the volunteer puts all the big rocks in the jar first and they all fit. The volunteer then puts the gravel in and all the gravel fits as it falls between the big rocks.

Here's where I "Greg-orize" the story a bit more.

Then the volunteer pours the sand in the container, but only half the sand fits, which prompts the volunteer to say, "HA! See it still didn't all fit!!"

The seminar leader replies, "It's ok. That wasn't the important stuff anyway. "

The fact is that without clear priorities, it's very possible that the people in your organization will end up wandering around in a gravel storm while bigger issues get lost in or left out of the process.

There's a pretty clear reason why this happens.

Gravel generates and represents activity. It makes people look busy and gives the impression that a lot is getting done when in fact it's more the case that a lot of low yield stuff is getting done. The trap here is that handling and managing a gravel storm takes a great deal of energy, so the people in the organization end up being exhausted while being plagued with the nagging feeling that the important stuff still didn't get done.

The words of the late Hall of Fame UCLA Basketball Coach John Wooden really say it all: "Don't mistake activity for achievement." (Jamison and Wooden, *Wooden: A Lifetime of Observation on and off the court*, 1997)

Focus on the "Big Rocks"!

Here's the rub, though - Before you can communicate the "Big Rocks" to the people in your organization, *you* must be clear on what the "Big Rocks" are.

If you aren't sure what the "Big Rocks" are, then it's time to start asking some questions and/or having some serious discussions to help you clearly establish your organizational priorities.

Additionally, consider conducting periodic "Big Rock Meetings" to help keep your team focused on what's most important and to communicate any shifts or changes in "Big Rocks". Also, make a point of running your decisions through a "Big Rock Filter" to ensure that the most important things drive your organization's every strategic move.

An organization that has everyone clear and focused on the "Big Rocks" is an organization that will be better positioned with team members who can confidently and competently make decisions that effectively move the goals and aims of the organization forward.

Leadership Reality Check #5
You can be looking at the same things and seeing something altogether different

I once had an employee in a retail setting who, regularly had a very disinterested facial expression when assisting customers. Customers sometimes even complained to me that he didn't seem like he cared.

I approached him with this and suggested that we role-play an interaction with a customer. During the role-play he demonstrated the same dour, disinterested facial expression that he exhibited when dealing with customers.

I said, "That was pretty good, but I need you to act more like you care about what the customer is saying". His reply was, "I *am* acting like I care about what you're saying" with the same dour, disinterested facial expression.

Situations like these can be particularly frustrating for leaders in that they are based in the leader and the team member having different and often times conflicting world views.

Another great example of this issue playing itself out in the real world came from a conversation I had with someone in attendance at one of my seminars.

During one of the breaks (which is, remember, where I usually learn the really interesting stuff) a lady approached me with a challenge she was faced with.

She had been recently promoted to the position of supervisor of a maintenance team on a university campus. The team she was now supervising was made up of people who had been her peers on the team before.

The challenge as she identified it was that she "wanted her team to take more pride in their work".

I asked her give me an example.

She said," For example when they clean up in the student's laundry room facility, they clean the top and front of the washers and dryers, but they never clean between them".

I asked her what it was that she wanted. She replied, "I want them to take more pride in their work!"

I asked her to give me an example. This time, with a greater sense of frustration (I could tell because she began to slow her rate of speech and really enunciate her words) she said, "I told you... when they clean up in the student's laundry room facility, they clean the top and front of the washers and dryers, but they never clean between them!!"

"So what do you want?" I asked.

She said, with a much more aggravated voice, "I want them to take more pride in their work".

I replied, "It doesn't sound like that to me. It sounds to me like you want them to clean between the washers and dryers. "

She began to laugh, as she got the point.

There's a really good chance that when she said to her team that she wanted them to take more pride in their work, they likely thought or even said out loud "We do take pride in our work!"

The point is that "pride in their work" wasn't the issue. The issue was how specifically she wanted them to clean the student's laundry area.

This happens all the time with leaders.

A sales manager, for example, tells their salesperson "I need you to sell more!"

When the sales report comes out the next day and the salesperson has sold 1 more widget (which, for the record, does qualify as "more"). The sales manager then approaches the salesperson and says I need you to sell "way more" than this.

Terms like "more" and "way more" are just about as helpful as asking people to "take pride in their work".

Other examples:

- Parents who want their children to "apply themselves more" in school
- Plant managers who want employees to "pay more attention to safety" in the workplace
- Leaders of civic organizations that want their members to "show more commitment"
- Principals who tell teachers they want them to "care more about the kids"

- Basketball coaches who want their team to "pick it up on defense"
- A wife who wants her husband to be "more affectionate"

All these are noble sentiments expressed with the best of intentions. But the truth is the kids could just as easily reply with "I *am* applying myself more", the plant workers may honestly counter that "they *are* paying more attention to safety", the members of the civic organization will likely energetically respond that they "*are* committed to the organization" and so on.

So how do we bridge this gap between what's desired and what's being delivered?

This reality check calls for a 2-part strategy.

Strategy Part I - Clarify Expectations
It's important to make sure that there isn't a gap between what you expect and what they think you expect. (Remember the index card test?)

Perhaps this disconnect is a signal that you may need to restate and/or clarify your expectations with your team.

Also, your people could be working on a previously determined set of expectations that aren't in alignment with yours. This can be a common occurrence when a leader takes over the reins of the organization or team from someone else.

In the case of the maintenance supervisor, it's completely within the realm of possibility that her predecessor never expressed a clear expectation that the employees should be making a point of cleaning between the washers and dryers.

This is why a great case can be made for having an expectations conversation with your new team right from the beginning. That means you should make no assumptions about what people should or should not know, or base any assumptions on how long someone's been doing something.

Strategy Part II – Provide feedback

As soon as you identify that there's a gap between your interpretation of how a job or task should be done and that of a member or members of your team, providing feedback is a critical component to helping point out where the disconnect is, why it's important to modify the behaviors in questions, and how to modify that behavior.

People tend to do things differently when they begin to see things differently. Feedback is the tool best suited to help team members see things differently.

Take note as we move through the book as to how many times feedback shows up as a strategy for helping your team members deliver the behaviors you need/want and you'll understand why we're dedicating an entire chapter (in fact, the largest chapter) of this book to the skill of delivering feedback effectively and efficiently.

Leadership Reality Check #6
Maybe your way isn't the best way

People often report in my seminars that team members don't do what you want because for any number of reasons, they believe that the strategy, tactic, procedure, or process you're suggesting won't work or that they have a better way.

When you run into this objection, there is a 2-part strategy that I suggest you put into play.

Strategy Part I - Listen
Why is the first part of a strategy designed to deal with the situation where your people believe your way won't work?

The answer is pretty simple - They may be right!

During Pathetica, I would have been hard pressed to embrace this strategy mainly because my humility, or really my lack of humility, would have prevented it.

To even consider that an employee of mine might be correct in assessing that some idea, process, or practice that I had deployed didn't actually work would have been unfathomable for me. To actually admit it would have been even more unlikely, to say the least.

Interestingly, my team picked up on this stubborn disposition of mine and rather than help shepherd the process in a different direction, they became content with just watching it fail.

Later, when the light of reality began to hit me, I actually had the nerve to approach the team with some asinine statement like,

"Why didn't someone tell me?" Their very legitimate response tended to be, "We tried to, but you wouldn't listen. "

So take (or avoid) a note from my Pathetica playbook, and when your team members tell you something's not working, take the time to listen *because they might be right.*

Strategy Part II - Provide Feedback
Once you've listened to what your team member(s) have to say, you'll realize that either:

1. They have a good point
2. You discover through your listening that there may be pieces of the puzzle that they are missing
3. There may be part(s) of how they are carrying out the assignment that need correction

When you listen first, you are better prepared to shape your feedback.

If, for example, you find through your listening that they have a good point, your feedback should reflect that. "Thanks for bringing that to my attention, I wasn't aware of that." or something along those lines would be the beginning of effective feedback on the issue.

If, however, after listening you detect that your team member(s) may be missing some understanding, making an error in how something is being done, etc. your feedback would take a very different tack. Something like, "I appreciate you bring that to my attention. I'm glad that you are focused on us succeeding. Going forward, let's make sure that when we do this we also take into account. . . "or something similar would be a great way to start an effective feedback conversation.

Again, we'll go into greater depth on how to effectively deliver feedback later in the book, but suffice it to say that delivering feedback whether they are correct in their assessment or not, provides you an opportunity to reinforce the behavior you want or develop alternative behaviors toward the ultimate goal of successfully focusing on your organization's "Big Rocks".

Here is bit more full disclosure from me on another error I made frequently during Pathetica.

I used both parts of this strategy when someone approached me with the idea that my way didn't work.

The only problem is that I reversed the parts.

In other words, I provided feedback on why I thought they were wrong first, and then I asked them what they had to say.

This didn't work very well in that the team member basically got from this approach that I was either trying to humiliate them to prevent future similar conversations, or that I wanted them to validate what I'd just said and the me-centered universe from which it was born; or maybe both.

In either case, the result of me reversing the parts of this strategy, providing feedback first and then asking for their input, usually resulted in them saying nothing at all; nothing to me, anyway.

Somehow, however, I'm certain that word of how I responded got back to the rest of the team, and so it was likely that I had created an environment where my entire team opted to hold their tongues rather than give me information critical to our success.

Actually, it's pretty reasonable to assume that this was so, because I can remember a time when I was treated in a similar fashion as an employee, and that's exactly how I responded - "Don't tell him! He'll figure it out soon enough on his own!"

So to summarize, after that wave of anecdotal rambling, when people think your way won't work or think they have a better way of doing something:

Strategy Part I - Listen (because they may be right)

Strategy Part II - Provide feedback based on what you heard.

Leadership Reality Check #7
People need to feel recognized and appreciated for good performance

As was the case with many issues, during Pathetica I had what I thought to be a very logical and sensible reply to any employee who dared mention any lack of reward or appreciation for doing their job.

I simply replied, "You get a check, don't you?! Do you not get a check every 2 weeks?!"

The problem with that retort, as I look back embarrassingly at it, was that if an effective reward or recognition system was as simple as my people getting a paycheck, then it follows that as long as they were getting a check, I should never have had a problem with them staying motivated and getting them to do what I needed them to do.

The fact is that all of us, to some degree, appreciate having our work acknowledged.

It's not necessarily because we need or require validation from others.

It's more the fact that it's nice to have your efforts and accomplishments noticed and more importantly, appreciated. And if you as a leader can deliver this in an audible/tangible way, that's all the better.

I've been struck over the years by how many people have stated in their own special way, that even to hear someone say, "thank you", would go a long way in keeping them motivated to do a good job.

When you hear sentiments like these from thousands of people from across cultures and from every demographic, there has to be something to it. It must be important, and if it's missing it could be subtly or seriously affecting your team's sustained level of performance.

Let's take a look at a 2-part strategy to help with this situation.

Strategy Part I - Provide Feedback
That's right! When people feel unappreciated one of the most effective ways to encourage and reinforce good behavior is by acknowledging it with your words.

Feedback serves as a tangible way for your team member(s) to know that you appreciate their efforts.

When it comes to feedback, however, we're talking about more than just saying, "Good Job!". While saying "Good Job!" certainly isn't a bad thing, it falls short of maximizing the feedback opportunity to ensure that the desired behavior will continue.

Effective feedback has a number of critical components that we'll go into in depth later in the book. For now, suffice it to say that your acknowledgement of a job well done will go a long way toward sustaining that performance. Doing so with effectively delivered feedback will do even more.

Strategy Part II - Create a meaningful recognition program (with emphasis on the word meaningful)
Note: Meaningful means meaningful to the *recipient* of the recognition.

I've heard countless stories about how differently the recipients of recognition and the givers of the recognition perceive the value of the recognition.

One of the biggest mistakes that many leaders make in giving recognition is that they gage how meaningful the recognition is by using their own personal yardstick. In other words, "If I like it, they should like it too. "

Let's take this for example.

My wife and I have 3 absolutely beautiful daughters. All of them have college degrees, 2 have earned Masters degrees, and at the time of this writing of this book, one is pursuing her Doctorate degree.

All three of them had financial assistance for the college and Masters degrees programs as a result of athletic and/or academic scholarships and graduate assistance programs (those of you who have or have had kids in college understand how big a deal this is financially for the family).

AND they are all gainfully employed and haven't moved back into the house... not yet anyway.

Not only have they achieved much, they are all genuinely good people. Not only do I love them, I like them (all parents will tell you that these two things don't always co-exist).

I've painted this picture for you because you'd think that these kids have lived their lives in such a way that it seems they would be deserving of some type of recognition from my wife and I.

Let's say my wife gave me the job* of finding a way to show them how proud we are of who they are and what they've accomplished.

*Note: While I am the CEO of my company, I am the "Acting" Assistant Supervisor at home.

So when all the girls come home for the holidays, I decide to sit them all down and summarize with great pride and love the story of their character and their accomplishments, and then say to them, "Because you've all 3 lived your lives with high character, a great work ethic, and because you're such all around quality people, your mom and I have decided to show you our appreciation. In recognition of who you've become, we have decided to give each of you. . . . [drum roll please] your own individual socket set, each with a lifetime warranty and your initials engraved on the case!"

[Sound of crickets chirping]

Chances are that while I feel it's a great gift and something that everyone needs and should have; it probably wouldn't go over very well with my daughters.

The truth is that there are a lot of leaders out there giving out virtual "socket sets" as tokens of their appreciation and in recognition of good performance.

The moral to my story, and possibly to your story as well, is that when there is a disconnect between how the giver and the recipient feel about the meaningfulness or value of the recognition, it usually results in two problematic outcomes.

- The recipient of the recognition could end up feeling slighted or unappreciated
- The giver of the recognition could end up feeling that the recipient is being unappreciative and ungrateful

This type of mutual resentment around recognition can have a substantially adverse and long term affect on the relationships within your team.

The real question is how do you make sure the recognition passes the "Meaningful" test.

It's such an important question that we've dedicated an entire chapter in this book to answering it, so read on my friend. Read on!

Leadership Reality Check #8
Accountability matters... a lot

I'm sure there's no chance that there are people out there in business, sports, or relationships who are not doing what is expected of them and not experiencing any consequence as a result (he said sarcastically).

The fact is that it happens all the time.

When people don't do what we want and or need them to do and experience nothing in the form of a consequence for that choice, what we've done in essence is to license the very behavior we don't want.

What's worse is that when you license the behavior (with an absence of consequences) for one person, you could actually be licensing the behavior for others on your team as well.

As soon as one person discovers that they can fail to comply with your wishes without consequences, chances are that there will be an informal meeting held with other members of the team - and you won't be invited.

That very short and informal meeting will go something like this:

"Look. . . I didn't do what he/she/they wanted, and nothing happened to me so what are you worried about?"

If you're not careful what was only one person on your team being non-compliant can soon become an epidemic of people on your team being non-compliant.

There are 2 strategies to employ when there is a perceived lack of consequences for non-compliant behavior.

Strategy Part I - Provide feedback

There's that "feedback" word again. But can feedback actually serve as a consequence for non-compliant behavior?

Absolutely!

Feedback can actually serve as one of the most powerful consequences because no one really cares to hear that they may have fallen short of your expectations of them.

Now we're not talking about chastisement, or berating verbal assaults; anything but.

What we are talking about is creating an environment where people know that if they aren't meeting your expectations that they'll hear about it.

Feedback only works well as a consequence that actually has an enduring impact on changing behavior if, when delivered it meets certain standards.

Here's the place where I say again, "We'll discuss how to deliver effective and efficient feedback later in the book." But then you probably saw that coming didn't you?

Strategy Part II - Deliver the appropriate consequences

It's important that you don't overdo or under do the consequences you deliver for non-compliant behavior. But that's often very much easier said than done.

Let's start by discussing why leaders so often over-do, under-do, or not-at-all-do consequences when faced with non-compliant behavior.

When we are too heavy handed in the delivery of consequences, it's often because we've allowed the behavior to persist to the point where our frustration gets the better of us and we overreact.

When we tread too lightly in the consequences we deliver (or don't deliver) it's often because we are trying to minimize the possibility of confrontation or conflict or we're trying to avoid hurting someone's feelings because "they're doing the best they can".

Sometimes we don't deliver consequences at all because we're "too busy to deal with that right now" or because "it wasn't that big a deal anyway".

To make sure the consequences we're delivering are "appropriate", there are 3 things we can do.

1. Deal with the non-compliant behavior as soon as you encounter it to minimize the chance that you'll be perceived as tolerating the behavior and to help prevent the chance that you'll build pent-up frustration that may lead to an inappropriate response on your part.
2. Understand that as the leader of your team not only do you have a right, but you also have a responsibility to make sure the members of your team are exhibiting behaviors that are moving the mission of your team forward.
3. If you are uncertain as to what "appropriate" consequences are, consider consulting a Human Resources professional to help you sort through what your options are. This could be a significant step to take as inappropriate consequences can not only lead to bad feelings and continued non-compliant behavior, they could have negative legal ramifications as well.

Leadership Reality Check #9
Behaviors that are rewarded are repeated – including the ones you don't want

When I start to bring this up in my seminars initially it evokes a response of general disbelief. Seminar attendees rarely think that they reward behaviors that they don't want. After a few seconds however, reality begins to sink in and what were looks of disbelief slowly morph into looks of quiet resignation.

Here are a few examples of what it might look like to reward someone for not doing what you want them to do:

- You have an employee on your payroll who regularly and over an extended period of time isn't doing what you want or need them to do and yet you keep them on your payroll.
- You have a player on your defensive minded basketball team that regularly fails to get back on defense or play in the defensive sets you've called, and you continue to allow them to be a starter on your team.
- Your child fails to do their assigned chores around the house, but continues to get the same kid perks (cell phone, movie trips, etc) as the rest of your children who are actually regularly doing their chores
- A member of your organization hasn't paid membership fees in the last few years, but still enjoys all the privileges of membership as your dues paying members.

All these examples and many more were actually shared with me by seminar attendees across industries and demographic lines.

The danger here, similar to the situation of there being no consequences for non-compliant behavior, is that rewarding non-compliant behavior not only emboldens the individual in question to continue their unacceptable behavior - it can also over time impact the culture of your organization.

It may slowly become the norm for people to either ignore or otherwise fail to comply with your expectations.

Not only can this impact your organization's performance, it can also become an H. R. nightmare in that it is very difficult to address behavior that you have condoned or even rewarded in the past.

So what's a leader to do?

Consider these 2 strategies.

Strategy # 1 - Clarify expectations
Here we are back at expectations again!

Reviewing and/or clarifying expectations is a critical first step, because it gives the person in question the maximum benefit of the doubt. Perhaps they are not (or are no longer) totally clear on what you expect.

This is not a "cop out" to avoid confrontation. It's very possible over time that the clarity of your expectations may have become cloudy.

This is an opportunity to review your expectations in detail. This is just to make sure there is no miscommunication or misinterpretation of your expectations.

Strategy # 2 - Communicate the consequences of continued non- compliance

Make sure this person, who has now been given the benefit of the doubt, understands what *specific* consequences can be expected if their behavior does not change.

Statements like these outline the specific consequence that a person can expect as a result of continued non-compliant behavior:

"You may face a written reprimand"
"You'll no longer be in the starting line-up. "
"You'll lose your cell phone privileges"

"You will no longer be able to attend member social events"On the other hand, statements like the ones that follow seem to convey that there may be consequences, but because the messaging is vague, the person may fail to take the potential consequences seriously:

"There could be some consequences"
"I might have to consider some changes"
"You might lose some privileges"
"It may limit what you can do within the organization"

Bottom line: Make sure that the specific consequences that can be expected for continued non-compliant behavior are clearly communicated and understood.

Leadership Reality Check #10
The Law of Unintended Punishment

If you think asking people to consider that they are rewarding unacceptable behaviors gets odd looks in a seminar, it's nothing compared to the looks I get when I suggest that they may be punishing people who are complying with what they need done.

Most people can't imagine a scenario in which they could be punishing compliant behavior, but it happens all the time and in a variety of ways.

Let's discuss some of the ways that a leader could be unintentionally punishing people for compliant behavior.

Potential Punishment # 1 - Burnout
All leaders of teams pretty quickly determine who the "go to" person is on their team. This is the person, when push comes to shove, can always be counted on to come through.

Here's the problem, though:

The "go to" person, initially anyway, considers the "go to" role to be a real compliment. It's a testament to the confidence of the leader's faith in their skill and dependability. They get special assignments and projects to work on, may stand in for the leader in a meeting, could be tasked with handling complex customer escalations, etc.

While the "go to" person is honored by this vote of confidence, he or she will likely notice that the number of extra tasks, assignments, and stand-ins will, over time, begin to increase at an ever quickening pace.

The net result is that the person who was at one time pleased and honored with the "go to" role quickly finds himself or herself on the road to burn out.

The "go to" person will probably also notice that their extra workload is coming "off the plate" of other members of the team.

In one fell swoop the leader has rewarded one person who's not getting the job done by removing tasks from them while at the same time punishing the "go to" person by increasing their workload (often without affecting their level of compensation and/or recognition).

If this happens, rest assured that feelings of resentment towards the leader are soon to follow.

Potential Punishment # 2 - Ostracism
It is possible that in addition to the "go to" person feeling burned out, that another perceived punishment could begin to take hold.

As the "go to" person gains more tasks, responsibilities, and opportunities, their peers can begin to see all this activity as "perks" reserved for the leader's virtual "teacher's pet". This can lead to resentment of the leader and by extension, unfortunately, the "go to" person.

This resentment could lead to strained relationships with co-workers/teammates, and in some cases could, as has been communicated to me by seminar attendees, lead to outright ostracism of the "go to" person by their peers.

In effect, the "go to" person can become isolated which can no doubt affect team cohesion and ultimately affect team productivity.

Potential Punishment # 3 – Micromanagement: "That's not how I would do it!"

One example of this punishment came from a fellow who attended one of my seminars.

He related that his wife had been expressing her discontent with his lack of support in keeping the house clean - particularly the kitchen.

After coming to the conclusion that she had a good point, he started making an effort to clean up the kitchen after she retired for bed each evening so that in the morning she'd wake up to a spotless kitchen.

One evening as he was cleaning the kitchen, she got up and came to the kitchen for a glass of water and noticed that he was cleaning and wiping down the kitchen surfaces using a cleanser and paper towels (vs. kitchen towels or sponges).

His wife, in his words, "scolded" him for being so wasteful as to use paper towels and that he should know better, and then set about the task of showing him how "she" cleaned the kitchen.

Interestingly, he stated that "how" he cleaned the kitchen hadn't been an issue for the 2 weeks prior during which he was doing his twilight cleaning because it was always done after his wife had gone to bed. It wasn't until she saw *how* he was doing it that things got a little sticky.

His response, admittedly out of spite, was to pull back on his efforts to keep the house clean, and as you might imagine a bad situation quickly became worse.

Another funny example was told to me by a woman in the audience who described a situation where there had been a falling out that took place between her husband and their son.

The father had tasked the son with making sure the lawn was cut every week.

Unbeknownst to the father, the son had (from money he earned from his part time job) been paying a neighborhood kid to mow the lawn when his dad was out playing golf.

The father, upon learning of this, was furious and grounded his son for a month.

While the mom did eventually get the son's sentence commuted, the injury to the father and son's relationship took a while to heal.

The moral to the story is that the Father gave the son an "objective" (lawn is mown once a week), but not a blueprint (son does the actual mowing) and even though the son actually accomplished the objective, he was punished.

Potential Punishment # 4 – No Acknowledgment of Effort
Here's another powerful example of where someone received what he or she perceives to be punishing behavior after doing what they were asked to do.

A woman mentioned that she'd recently had a contentious conversation with her husband about his desire for her to "spruce herself up a bit". He told her that he wanted her to wear make-up more often and lose some weight.

While it hurt her feelings, because their relationship had been struggling lately, she decided to take steps to try to respond to his request.

Her punishment, as she felt it, was that after her efforts her husband never said a word to her acknowledging the effort that she was putting forth in response to his request that she "spruce herself up a bit".

That he didn't seem to notice or worse even acknowledge her effort to her felt like a punishment.

One more typical punishment – Meetings that start late

There is another very common punishment for people doing what you want them to do. I hear about it in some shape form or fashion from nearly every client I work with.

They express frustration with the fact that people don't show up on time for meetings, and as a result the day's schedule is thrown off track.

Where is the punishment factor in this, you ask?

The recipients of punishment in this scenario are the people who actually show up on time for meetings. In fact, every minute that passes beyond the published meeting start time serves to make the punishment that much greater.

Interestingly, when you ask people privately why they don't show up on time for meetings, the universal response is "They never start on time anyway!" In other words, every time a meeting doesn't start at the appointed time it sends a signal to attendees that the stated start time is a relative concept and wholly unimportant.

If you track this closely, you'll find that the people who are habitually late for meetings were, at one time, people who actually used to show up on time only to find themselves sitting there waiting for the late starting meeting to begin. They eventually begin to see the effort that they made to be on time as wasted effort and modified their behavior accordingly.

Ironically, the people responsible for getting the meeting started usually delay the meeting so that the late arriving people won't miss anything. By delaying the start of the meeting, they are actually rewarding the behavior of those who aren't arriving on time, not delivering any consequences for their showing up late, and punishing the people who actually made it on time – all at the same time.

A very similar conversation could be had around people who meet/miss deadlines.

So how do we avoid creating an environment where people feel punished for doing what we want them to do?

There are a number of strategies that might be useful when dealing with situations like these.

Strategy # 1 - Replace the "go to" person's punishment with reward

Acknowledge the "go to" person not only with extra tasks and opportunities but also with words of appreciation and, where warranted, compensation that is commensurate with the "beyond and above" work that you're giving them.

Strategy # 2 - Hold team members accountable
Hold everyone in the organization accountable for his or her work and responsibilities and avoid removing work from the table of non-compliant team members and placing it on the table of your compliant team members.

Strategy # 3 - Avoid the specter of favoritism
Make it clear in your organization "why" your "go to" person is your "go to" person.

Outline what it is that they "do" that makes you confident in their ability to handle additional tasks and responsibilities and reassure other team members that similar behaviors on their part might lead to additional opportunities and responsibilities for them as well.

Strategy # 4 - Be clear on whether the objective or the steps toward the objective, (or both) is what's important to you
If your team members are accomplishing the objectives you've set out for them, but aren't doing it the way you would have done it, "WHO CARES?!"

Leave them alone, or better yet acknowledge their innovative approach and successful achievement of the assigned objective.

Unless the steps they follow to accomplish the objective you assigned have a negative impact on other aspects of your mission or create an untenable cost or expense, don't worry about it.

If there are reasons that the blueprint they decided to work with are problematic for the organization, take the time to explain in specific terms what the unintentionally negative consequences of their approach were and then provide them with a blueprint to follow going forward. As much as possible, leave room in the prescribed blueprint for innovation and creativity.

Sounds a lot like feedback, huh?

Strategy # 5 - Acknowledge effort and incremental progress

Avoid waiting for your team members to "cross the finish line" before acknowledging their effort and progress along the way.

If people are on the right road and making progress along that road, a word of acknowledgement and encouragement from the leader goes a long way toward sustaining that positive momentum.

Strategy #6 – Start Meetings on Time

When it becomes clear to people in your organization that meetings will start on time with or without them, it will only take a meeting or 2 before you begin to see a shift in the punctuality paradigm.

At the same time, you'll also be sending a subliminal but powerful message about timeliness (whether it's related to meetings or deadlines) in general.

Leadership Reality Check #11
You will one day have to deal with insubordination

During "Pathetica" I had not yet considered nor was I even aware of how many reasons there could be for non-compliant behavior.

As a result, my default response to anything that did not seem to fall in the category of "training needed" was that the person wasn't doing what I wanted them to do because they were being willfully defiant or insubordinate.

I know this sounds woefully ignorant on my part, and it was - ignorant not as in stupid, but ignorant as in uninformed.

My lack of understanding in this regard is probably why, during "Pathetica", I hated the H. R. Department.

Now I know that hate is a pretty strong word, but I felt that way because everything I tried to do to deal with poor performance was constantly being overturned and was therefore, in my way of thinking at the time, totally undermining my authority as a manager.

I and a couple of other managers who'd not yet emerged from "Pathetica" used to remark that the people in H. R. turned our problem employees into boomerangs – you throw them out and they come right back to you.

It wasn't until I emerged from the darkness of "Pathetica" that I realized the folks in H. R. were actually not only protecting the company from my poor decisions – they were protecting me as well.

Now that the really long preamble is complete, let's be clear as to what I mean by insubordination.

Insubordination, as I'm describing it, is when someone refuses to do what you've asked in a stand of outright defiance.

Here's an example from my own personal experience.

I once had an employee whose name I will not disclose (even though I am no longer afraid of him) with whom I had a classic insubordination clash.

Here's how the conversation went:

Me: "I need you to make a follow up call to this customer to gather some additional information on the technical problems she's having. "

Employee: "I'm not going to do that. "

* After an awkward pause, I begin to justify my request *

Me: "It's very important that we get this information from this customer, and since you are the person who spoke to her initially, you're the best person to follow up. "

Employee: "I said I'm not going to do that. "

* An even more awkward pause *

Me: "I'm not sure why you're taking this so personally, but I'm not kidding around here. This is part of your job. I need you to make this call right away!"

Employee: "What part of 'I'm not going to do that' don't you understand?"

After a few moments of very tense silence, I walked away from this employee's desk and went straight over to the desk of my "go to" person and said, "There's something I need you to take care of for me…"

My way of dealing with the insubordination was to let the insubordinate employee off the hook (in an attempt to end the impasse and conflict) and take the work over to the person who I was already beginning to burn out with an ever-growing workload.

Something tells me that there was probably an informal team gathering held shortly after this event during which the insubordinate employee conducted a very short training seminar that went something like this:

Mr. Insubordinate: "If you don't want to do something, just tell him you're not going to do it. He'll leave you alone after a while. "

Chances are everyone on the team will have been invited to this informal training seminar except for two people – my "go to" person and me.

I hope you've never encountered an incidence of insubordination as severe as the one I've recounted here. But chances are, if you're in a position of leadership long enough, I can pretty much guarantee you that one day, it'll be your turn.

So what's a leader to do when faced with what is clearly insubordination?

Begin the process of reducing the number of passengers on the bus (start taking the steps necessary to get them off your team).

When it becomes clear to you that a member of your team has made the willful decision to defy your directives, there is a prescriptive approach that is found in virtually every H. R. Manual for organizations, public and private and it goes something like this:

Insubordination is grounds for immediate corrective action or progressive discipline up to and including termination/dismissal/removal.

It is probably, on the surface, the most clear-cut of any of the strategies we've discussed so far.

The real question is that if it's so clear and widely accepted as a response to insubordination, why isn't it employed more often?

I submit that there are likely a number of reasons including, but not limited to, those listed here:

1. Fear of conflict or confrontation
2. To take the steps associated with progressive disciplinary action up to and including termination, it's critical to be able to produce clear documentation to justify the decision and the fact is that many leaders don't know how to or just haven't taken the time to document these behaviors in a way that allows the decision (especially in the case of termination, dismissal, or removal) to hold up under the

scrutiny of accepted H. R. principles and/or employment and labor laws.

3. In volunteer based organizations, the leverage of "job" action does not exist in the same way. As a result, the organization's leadership feels powerless to act.

4. The leader feels that because of what they perceive to be a massive amount of red tape in their organization to take such a job action, it just isn't worth the time or trouble.

5. The leader feels that the decision to dismiss or remove the person will not be supported by the organization and would lead to a reversal of his or her decision. The result of which would be the leader's perception that it would end in him or her losing face or legitimacy with the team.

6. If the situation is family related, how do you "fire" family?

These are very real issues that face leaders across organizations every single day.

If you come to the conclusion that it's time for you to take more stringent measures in the form of progressive discipline and or termination/dismissal/removal you might want to keep the following in mind:

Don't ignore it or put off dealing with it.
Ignoring it or putting it off because of a worry about conflict or an aversion to jumping through the requisite administrative hoops will not make the insubordinate behavior go away. It will more likely embolden the behavior and license it for other members of your team. Deal with the situation expeditiously. As uncomfortable as it might be, it comes along with the responsibility of leadership.

Keep good records
Take copious notes and document instances of insubordination - including dates, times, and the detailed circumstances surrounding the occurrence.

Consult H. R.
Consult an H. R. Professional before acting to ensure that you aren't putting your organization or yourself in legal jeopardy.

Be proactive
Especially if you're a volunteer based organization, it's important to publish and communicate your policies around what are considered appropriate and inappropriate behaviors in the organization. This diminishes the "nobody ever told me that" defense to insubordinate behavior (yep, people will try most anything).

This may be difficult to believe, but some people are actually relieved to have you escort them off the bus, because they were probably miserable in the job.

I often poll my audience as to how many people had to take the step to terminate an employee before. Most people raise their hands.

Then I ask how many people had an employee actually thank them for terminating them. A considerable number of hands go up in the affirmative – including my own.

It's hard for some to believe, but sometimes the behaviors you see are more than a sign of defiance. Those behaviors are just as often a sign of unhappiness with the current job. Sometimes the person just doesn't know how to walk away.

When as a leader you take the steps to remove a person from the bus, the result, for some people, is a profound sense of relief.

This may be hard to believe, but it's true nonetheless.

Oh... and in the case of an insubordinate family member:

If the family member is an employee, then in the workplace, you should treat them as such. This means that they don't get a pass when it comes to insubordinate behavior.

If it turns out, as I have heard from some seminar attendees, that the family member in question is "untouchable" because they are the owner's child, aunt, cousin, spouse, etc. , then you are only left with 2 options, really:

1. Deal with it
2. Find another job

If it's your child being insubordinate in your home, you should consider that behavior to be wholly unacceptable (in other words, stop making excuses for it, parents – otherwise you're setting your children up for a very tough life lesson later on), and if it happens it should result in the immediate long-term consequences including the shutdown of all privileges and perks.

If it's your 30-year-old child (or some other family member) who is still living in your home and they exhibit insubordinate behavior, they need to immediately begin the process of finding another bus (address) to ride on.

If it's your spouse, and you're the husband, just do what you're told and then slowly back your way out of the room.

Leadership Reality Check # 12
Some people just aren't cut out for some things

I'm a pretty optimistic guy. I believe that most anyone can achieve most anything they set their mind to.

But I'm also a realist in that I know that some people just aren't cut out for some things.

For example, it has become clear to me that some people should never, under any circumstances whatsoever, ever be allowed to speak to or in any way interact with customers or clients – *ever.*

In some cases, they shouldn't even be allowed to make eye contact with the people your organization serves because even the slightest contact with these folks often results in irate customers and sometimes disgruntled teammates as well.

This doesn't mean that, by definition, they are bad people. They should just never be put in customer facing positions.

Similarly, there are some people who should not work in finance, some should not be placed in positions where high-level organizational skills are required, and quite frankly there are some who should probably not be placed in supervisory or management positions.

Again, this is not because they are by nature bad or inept people, necessarily. Some jobs, tasks, or responsibilities are just not a good fit for everyone.

So what do you do when you come to the conclusion that someone in your organization is in a poor fit for his or her skill set or personal temperament?

Consider the following strategies as viable options.

Strategy # 1 – Move them to a position in your organization that is more in line with their skills and temperament.
There are a few caveats to this strategy, however.

Caveat # 1 to moving them to another position
You should only move them to another position in your organization that is more in line with their skills and temperament ***if*** such a position exists.

Avoid making the oft repeated mistake of just moving them to get them out of the job they are in at present.

This often just results in moving the problem to another part of the organization.

If I had a nickel for every time someone told me a story about how a person was simply moved to another department or position within the organization only to wreak havoc at his or her new organizational address, I'd be able to give away this book for free.

If this person is not a good fit anywhere in your organization, it's time to begin the process of reducing the number of passengers on the bus.

Caveat # 2 to moving them to another position
If they aren't a good fit in their current role, for goodness sakes, don't promote them just to get them off that team or out of that role.

If I had a penny for every time I've heard and/or seen this happen, I could pay you to read this book and still make a substantial profit.

If a person is wreaking havoc in their current role because it isn't a good fit, don't give them a broader role and allow them to wreak havoc on a grander scale.

Again, if this person is not a good fit anywhere in your organization, it's time to begin the process of reducing the number of passengers on the bus.

Caveat # 3 to moving them to another position
Don't assign them to "special projects" just to get them out of the picture.

I'm not sure when the strategy of assigning individuals who don't fit well anywhere in the organization to "special projects" began.

It's like putting the person in "organizational limbo" so that you can minimize the damage they can do to the organization without having to take the more difficult step of removing them from the bus. (By the way, this falls under the category of rewarding the behavior you don't want).

Sending this person to "Organizational Siberia" (no offense intended to Siberians) can actually send an interesting signal to the rest of the members of your organization, most of whom understand exactly what the "special projects" move was all about.

It says "we don't know what to do with him or her, so we're just going to put them in the corner where they can't do harm to themselves or others".

Again, and this time with feeling, if this person is not a good fit anywhere in your organization, it's time to begin the process of reducing the number of passengers on the bus.

Strategy # 2 – Revisit, review, and if necessary revise your hiring or selection filter.

It could be that your organization is trending toward team members being in positions that are not a good fit.

I find that with some of my clients it has been a while since they took a look at their job descriptions and the skill sets necessary to execute those jobs.

As a result, even the organization's interview processes can become compromised in terms of effectiveness in the selection of the right candidates for the right positions.

For example, 10 years ago, "Job A" may not have required very extensive skills, if any, with regards to building or understanding data spreadsheets, but today that skill is essential to the successful ability to proficiently handle "Job A's" requisite responsibilities.

Make it a priority ("Big Rock") to regularly assess the necessary skills and temperament critical to the various roles in your organization. In so doing, be willing to recalibrate your selection criteria and training vehicles to stay current and successful in moving your organization's mission forward with sustained operational excellence.

Leadership Reality Check #13
Sometimes what you want isn't realistic

Let's face it; sometimes the work stack gets too high for any one individual to effectively deal with.

This is often the result of not regularly taking a "30,000 foot view" of the organization in general, and of individual workloads in particular.

A great example of this was a story shared with me by a fellow who started an insurance agency from scratch (with zero clients) 3 years earlier.

Because of his commitment to creating a great customer experience, his list of clients ballooned to more than 1000 in just 2 years.

He'd made a habit of contacting every one of his clients at least once a year to review their coverages and ensure that they were adequately protected. He also called them on their birthdays and to let them know about new products and services that may benefit them. He'd set a standard to answer all calls within 2 rings, and hand delivered policies to clients who were unable to come into the office – all while continuing to build his clientele through a very innovative and successful referral program.

The challenge, he soon discovered, was that it was easier to meet these service standards with one employee when he had 300 clients. Not so easy however when his business reached 1000 clients and was still growing.

Suddenly, it seemed to his clients that the level of service that they'd grown accustomed to had begun to deteriorate. This was the case even though the agency owner and his employee were working harder than ever.

The story of this agent's challenge is not at all uncommon. A workload that was at one time manageable for he and his employee had, ironically, become unmanageable because of his level of success.

Simply put, he had more work to be done that he had resources to do that work. Especially if he wanted to maintain the now expected level of service to which his clients had become accustomed.

So what could he do, and what can you do when faced with a similar dilemma?

Reassess your resources

When the balance of your resources and your critical organizational tasks begin to reach a point of diminishing return, it's time to reassess the size, scope, and type of resources you need to keep things on track.

This can be done in a number of ways.

1. Explore whether there is technology that can help streamline processes and tasks that don't require a human touch.
2. Review organizational priorities to make sure that the most important things aren't falling through the cracks
3. Employ external resources or stop gap measures to help support the workload and/or increase organizational efficiency (like hiring me – shameless plug)

4. Recalibrate your distribution of work, when necessary
5. Seriously consider hiring additional staff to handle the increased workload

Many organizations struggle with # 5 in the list above because of a concern about the expense associated with hiring additional staff.

This insurance agent I referenced earlier addressed this concern with what I thought was a very progressive way of thinking.

He chose to think of his employee complement as an investment rather than an expense. That paradigm allowed him to set about the task of systematically assessing what he could lose (clients) vs. what he could gain (clients and more referrals) by adding staff. The result was that he hired an additional full-time employee and a part-time employee.

When last he and I spoke his client base had grown to more than 3,000 and his agency was experiencing record levels of growth, customer satisfaction, client referrals, productivity, and profitability. Not bad!

Make sure that you, as a leader, are regularly reassessing your resources as they relate to you team members' workloads. Then make sure to balance what you discover against what you need to successfully achieve your operational goals.

CHAPTER 3

THE NON-COMPLIANCE FILTER

There is an outside chance that you may be thinking, "I was struggling when I thought there were only a few leadership reality checks to be aware of! With all of these possibilities listed in the last chapter, how will I know what's really going on?" Well perhaps those were not your exact thoughts, but maybe I was close.

Either way, it would be a fair question. To help you answer it, I've devised a tool that I'd like to share with you. It's called the "Non-Compliance Filter". You'll see it on the pages that follow.

The Non-Compliance Filter

Name: _____

Desired Behavior: _____

Date of Assessment: _____

Are you *absolutely, positively* certain that…

❑ **They have the skills necessary to do the task?**
If not, schedule the appropriate training as soon as possible.

❑ **They know your precise expectations?**
If not, schedule a time to clearly communicate your expectations.

❑ **They understand how the task fits into the "Big Picture"?**
If not, schedule a time to discuss how the task fits into the larger scheme of the operations of the organization.

❑ **Their tasks are clearly prioritized?**
If not, schedule a meeting to communicate what the "Big Rocks" are for the person in question and immediately communicate any changes to the "Big Rock" list. Consider holding weekly "Big Rock" meetings.

❑ **They aren't right in thinking your way won't work or that their way won't work better?**
Schedule a time to listen to why they've come to that conclusion and then give them feedback relative to what they've shared with you. Use the "20 Foot Rule".

❑ **There is a reward/appreciation for doing what you want?**

If not, make sure you're giving ample feedback and that you have a meaningful recognition program.

❑ **Non-Compliant behavior is being met with the appropriate consequences?**

If not, make sure you're giving ample feedback and that you know how to execute the appropriate consequences for the behavior in question.

❑ **They aren't being rewarded for *not* doing the task?**

If not, make sure you establish/re-establish a culture of accountability.

❑ **They aren't being punished for doing what you want?**

If not, make sure you aren't contributing to the "burn out factor" by overloading your "go to" person.

❑ **You've accurately identified and are dealing appropriately with insubordinate behavior?**

If not, make sure that you haven't misidentified another reason as insubordination. If you have accurately identified their behavior or lack thereof as insubordinate, ensure that you are taking the appropriate measures including corrective action and progressive discipline.

❑ **The task or job is a good fit for this individual?**

If not, look to utilize this individual in a role that is more in line with their skills and abilities. . . if such a role exists.

❑ **Your expectations are reasonable?**

If not, rethink your expectations and/or recalibrate your distribution of work and/or rethink whether you have adequate resources.

Here's how to use the filter.

You'll notice at the top you're asked to enter the name of the person in question, the behavior that you're looking for or having problems with, and the date that you're making this assessment.

Then you'll see the words "Are you **absolutely, positively** certain that..." followed by a list of statements and their requisite strategies. For example, with the first statement the question is "Are you absolutely, positively certain that the person has the skills necessary to do the task?"

If you can definitively answer yes to the question, then place a checkmark in the box at the beginning of the statement. If there is even a shred of doubt about whether the answer is a definitive yes, leave the box unchecked. Remember your answer should not be based on how long they've been doing the task or whether "they should know". Your answer should be based as best you can on the facts, as you know them.

Then take the same approach to all the rest of the statements on the Non-Compliance Filter.

When you make it through the entire list of statements, you will no doubt have some boxes checked and some not. Every box you left unchecked has now become an action item for you to follow up on with that individual.

The Non-Compliance Filter allows you to take a strategic approach to getting the behaviors you need or want.

Hints, Tips, and Suggestions for using the "Non-Compliance Filter"

Hint/Tip/Suggestion #1

If you have a person that has more than one desired behavior that you're looking for and not getting, fill out a separate Non-Compliance Filter form for **each behavior in question**. It may be that you need different strategies for different situations.

The same strategies may not work or even be appropriate for the different behaviors. Completing a different form for each behavior will help you isolate the issues and strategies you'll need to take for each behavior.

Hint/Tip/Suggestion #2

If you're not sure what the answer is to the questions asked in each statement, consider consulting that person to get their input on the answer as well.

For example if you're not certain about whether the person is crystal clear on your expectation, you might ask them, "How clear do you feel you are about what I expect of you?" You could also do the index card expectations exercise we discussed under Leadership Reality Check#3 earlier in the last chapter.

In effect, I'm suggesting you use the 20 Foot Rule (see the next chapter) when you run into statements for which you are uncertain about the answer.

Hint/Tip/Suggestion #3

The Non-Compliance Filter has at it's core the purpose of helping you get the person in question on track as a consistently performing member of your team.

If you approach it with that mindset, it will likely be much more helpful for you and for them.

Hint/Tip/Suggestion #4

If you take a pretty good look at the filter, you'll recognize it as the same slate of questions you may get from you H. R. department if you're considering a job action of some type.

In other words, the Non-Compliance Filter is pretty similar to the H. R. Filter when it comes to you taking a justifiable and defensible disciplinary or corrective action with the person in question.

Let me see if I can be even plainer. If you go though the entire filter and:

1. You have checkmarks in every box, and
2. You are still not getting the behavior you desire

It may be time to begin the process of reducing the number of passengers on the bus.

Hint/Tip/Suggestion #5

Many attendees of my seminars find the Non-Compliance Filter to be very useful.

As a result, I've actually created a pdf of the Non-Compliance Filter that has all the questions on one page.

If you think it might be helpful, please go to this sp\
my website: **http://greggray. com/gtst**

There you'll find a downloadable version of the Non-Co\
Filter and other forms that you can use to your heart's co ⌐nt.

CHAPTER 4

"THE 20 FOOT RULE"

Earlier in the book we discussed that sometimes people may believe that your way of doing things won't work or that they have a better way of doing things.

We also discussed how perplexing this was for me during "Pathetica" when I was thoroughly convinced that my employees had to be wrong because I, of course, had all the answers.

The primary strategy we identified when faced with such an issue was to listen... *because they might be right.* In other words, a willingness to listen is a key component to sustaining a successful operation of any type.

I had an experience that was a real eye opener on this point and it came in a chat I had with a nice lady named Van Eure back on February 11, 2001. Van was and still is the owner of a quaint little restaurant in Raleigh, NC called the "Angus Barn".

In this chat with Van, I heard one of the most elegantly simple and strikingly powerful approaches to employee engagement that I'd ever heard. And trust me on this – as a Customer

Service Warrior, I have a very high bar when it comes to evaluating customer service experiences.

Here's how the conversation took place.

I had just conducted my "Desperately Seeking Service" seminar for a client in the Raleigh, NC area. Later that day, the client just raved about this restaurant called the Angus Barn that was legendary in the area and invited me to dinner there to see what it was all about.

On the way over, I was informed that the Angus Barn was so popular that guests often flew in from across the country to dine there and visit their award winning Wine Cellar.

I also heard that if you had plans to dine at the Angus Barn on a Friday, you should probably plan 2-3 weeks ahead as it was so popular that it was often booked weeks ahead on some nights.

I also learned that not only was there a waiting list for customers to get into the Angus Barn, there was also a waiting list of prospective employees to work at the Angus Barn. That's right! The Angus Barn had, and still has, such a great reputation as a great place to work that scores of prospective employees put the Angus Barn on notice that if they were fortunate enough to be hired, they would leave their current job in a heartbeat.

Let me summarize what I've told you so far: Not only is there a line to get in the front door of the Angus Barn, there is also a line to come through the back door as an employee as well.

By the way, my dining experience at the Angus Barn stands as one of the best service experiences I've ever had, restaurant or otherwise, ever.

As a guy who makes a living doing seminars and consulting with companies on how to create a great customer experience, I've learned that often the real test of the organization isn't what happens when things are going well. Rather, the real test comes when things break down or when problems occur.

When I got the chance that evening to chat with Van, I asked her how she handles problems or issues with operations.

Without hesitation, she said, "Whenever we run into a problem around here, we use the 20 Foot Rule".

She said this in such a matter of fact manner that I was more than a little embarrassed that I didn't know what "The 20 Foot Rule" was. But not wanting to admit my ignorance (a side effect of testosterone) and in a totally unnecessary attempt to save face, I responded, "Soooo... when *you* use the 20 Foot Rule, how do *you* implement it?"

Van looked me right in the eye, chuckled and said, "You have no idea what the 20 Foot Rule is, do you Greg?"

I replied, "No Ma'am, I don't". (busted)

She then explained the 20 Foot Rule to me.

She said that whenever they run into a problem at the Angus Barn, the first thing they do is talk to all the people who work within 20 feet of the problem.

When I asked her why, she delivered one of the smoothest elevator speeches I've ever heard.

She said that they talked to the people who worked within 20 feet of the problem because:

1. They usually knew it was a problem before she knew it was a problem
2. They probably had already thought up a number of ways to solve the problem
3. Chances are that their solutions were probably going to be more cost effective than what she might come up with
4. Their solutions will likely be more relevant and practical since they are actually the ones who do the work
5. When you involve people in the problem solving process, they take more ownership in implementing the solutions

I then asked her how her employees react if a solution they suggest doesn't get implemented. She replied by telling me that it's not usually a big deal because everyone that works at the Angus Barn knows she is willing to listen.

So what has Van's approach to leadership at the Angus Barn yielded?

From AngusBarn. com:
Over 200 awards have been received by the Angus Barn over the last 40 years, including the prestigious Ivy, DiRöNA, Wine Spectator Grand and Fine Dining Hall of Fame Awards. "Angus Barn Tops in the Nation" ranked 29th among Top Grossing Independent Restaurant in the United States by Restaurant and Institutions Magazine, January 2000. It also was ranked the #2 Best Steak Restaurant in America by Wine Spectator.

Wow! The "20 Foot Rule" – Thank you Van Eure, owner of the Angus Barn!

Now contrast the Angus Barn's approach to some things that you've likely experienced when it comes to employee suggestions.

Like the suggestion box that you can't fit your suggestion into because it is packed full – mainly because it never gets emptied. Or how about the suggestion box that seems to have no bottom and is positioned directly above the trashcan.

So what's the lesson here?

If you want to not only reach, but sustain a level of operational excellence in your organization, you would be well advised to consider making Van Eure's simple but powerful "20 Foot Rule" a regular part of your leadership toolbox.

And next time you're going to be anywhere near Raleigh, NC and you want to see excellence in action, treat yourself to a visit at the Angus Barn. When you do, please tell Van Eure that Greg Gray said hello and "Thanks!" Oh, and do yourself a favor and call way ahead for a reservation!

In case you're wondering, here's the information for The Angus Barn:
The Angus Barn
9401 Glenwood Avenue
(Highway 70 at Aviation Parkway)
Raleigh, North Carolina 27617
919-781-2444
angusbarn. com

CHAPTER 5

COMMUNICATING CLEAR EXPECTATIONS

We've talked quite a bit about the importance of communicating clear expectations to the members of your team.

At every level of your organization there should be specific Big Rock activities and expectations to which team members are held accountable.

When outlining those expectations, it's easiest and most effective to think in terms of "What does this activity/outcome look like?"

When it comes to Big Rocks, it's okay to wax philosophical. However, when it comes to expectations relative to moving those Big Rocks you need to be able to describe observable, measurable, behaviors and the results you're looking for.

For example, let's say that one of your Big Rocks is being accessible to clients. The question then becomes as you begin to craft your expectations "What does that look like?"

- Office hours that are convenient
- Plenty of locations
- Customer access to management

For teachers, it might mean:

- Being available for parent teacher conferences
- Sharing an email address with parents to facilitate communication

For college professors it may mean:

- Having adequate office hours for student consultations.

If one of your Big Rocks is to make sure you're responsive to the people you serve, that might translate into the development of specific service standards, such as:

- Returning phone calls within 4 hours
- Replying to e-mails within 24 hours
- Answering phone calls within the 1st 2 rings

Sometimes the Big Rocks don't easily translate to every part of your organization. If that's the case in your organization, you're going to need to work a little harder at connecting the dots.

If, for example, creating a great customer experience is a Big Rock for your organization:

- What role does the maintenance/custodial staff play in creating a great customer experience?
- What role does your security team play in creating a great customer experience?
- What role do you as the leader play in creating a great customer experience?

Always, the big question to answer is "What does it look like?"

In effect, every expected activity that takes place in your organization should roll up to one or more of your organizational Big Rocks.

That's only half the job, however when it comes to expectations. It is equally important for you to communicate to your team how your expectations impact your organizational Big Rocks. If you can do this effectively you not only answer the "What?" question for your team, you answer the "Why?" question as well.

Remember that in some cases people aren't doing what you want them to do because they don't know why they should do it. When you clearly outline your expectations and effectively communicate why those expectations are in place and how they impact your Big Rock objectives, you're at the same time telling your team members how they themselves fit into the Big Picture. This will allow them to better understand the importance of their role in the organization. When that happens what you get is a team that is able to supply its own fuel for motivation.

Summary

- Clearly identify your organizational big rocks
- Determine how and why every level of your organization contributes to the organization's Big Rocks
- When defining expectations always look to answer the question "What does that look like?"

Make sure every team member clearly understands how what is expected of them ties to the Big Rocks.

Expectations and Adaptability

In the grand scheme of things your organizational Big Rocks represent your mission and vision. The expectations you communicate represent your strategies for getting the mission accomplished. A leader's responsibility is also to regularly monitor whether these strategies are working.

The trap that many leaders fall into is that they become *married* to strategies. This happens quite often when a particular strategy was the brainchild of the leader him or herself. If this happens, there can be a reluctance to adapt or abandon the strategy that, after having been given ample time and opportunity to work, has failed to produce results that move the Big Rocks or mission forward.

A quote attributed to the former Chairman of the Joint Chiefs of Staff and Secretary of State Colin Powell provides great advice for leaders in this regard:

"Don't hold your ego so close to your position that when your position falls, your ego goes with it." (Harari, *The Leadership Secrets of Colin Powell*, 2002)

Because a strategy fails doesn't mean the leader has failed, unless he or she is unwilling to course correct and look for a more successful strategy.

The advice I often give the clients is to write your mission and vision in *ink* but write your strategies in *pencil*.

Expectations and Performance Management Systems

Performance management systems, when well written and devised, are really performance expectations systems.

When an individual reviews his or her performance management system they should see a blueprint for the tasks, responsibilities, and goals for their particular position in the organization.

The performance management/expectation system for a particular role should be part of the person's initial orientation to that role.

Further, the job/role description for the position should be a reflection of the performance management/expectation system for that particular position

Interestingly, it is not unusual for employees to see their performance review management system for the 1st time when they are actually receiving their annual merit review. What seminar attendees often share (during the seminar breaks of course) is that one of the most interesting periods of time at the job is "review season". Review season is that time of year when annual performance reviews are given – often to all employees around the same time.

During review season there is a significant uptick in activity in these particular areas:

1. Supervisors and managers passing drafts of reviews back and forth with what seems to be an endless stream of edits.
2. Employees inquiring and comparing notes with each other and asking questions like "What did he or she put on your review?" (he or she being the supervisor or manager)

Review season is often such a busy season that it can even distract team members from being focused on the job at hand.

In this type of environment, the annual performance/merit review becomes an *event*. If this is allowed to happen, the effectiveness of the review in evaluating performance and driving/sustaining operational excellence can be compromised.

I'm editorializing a bit here, but I submit that if you want your performance management/expectation systems to be a help versus a hindrance as you seek to sustain operational excellence, there are a few steps I suggest you consider taking:

1. Clearly establish what the Big Rocks are for your organization.
2. Adopt organizational strategies to support the Big Rocks.
3. Translate those organizational strategies into departmental/division strategies at every level of the organization.
4. Translate those strategies into departmental/divisional *expectations*, taking care to describe what those expectations look like.
5. Translate departmental/divisional expectations into expectations for individual roles on your team, taking care to again describe what those expectations look like.
6. Import those expectations into a performance management expectations document for each role on your team.
7. Develop metrics to measure performance against expectations
8. Review performance relative to those expectations via a formal conversation with team members each month.
9. Roll those monthly performance reviews up into quarterly reviews.
10. Role those quarterly reviews up and into the annual review for the team member.

Employing a strategy like this will transform your performance reviews from being events to being part of an ongoing conversation about performance. It will also help you keep you and your team focused on sustained operational excellence.

Now my guess is that at least one person reading this is thinking, "I don't have time to do all this reviewing!"

My response, respectfully, is what else is more important?

Chances are that you, like many leaders, spend a lot of time putting out fires as you react to one crisis after another. I wonder how many of those fires and crises could've been prevented with a more proactive approach to leadership.

Here's a pointed question on performance management and expectation systems; if you use such systems, when was the last time you compared what was on your reviews with what happens currently in the real world?

It isn't uncommon for review systems to be constructed, which takes a considerable amount of time mind you, and then not revisited in some cases for years.

The actual review delivery, as a result, ends up being retrofitted into a system that is no longer up-to-date, or in some cases no longer even relevant to the organization.

It takes a considerable amount of time and effort to review and if necessary, revise performance management/expectation systems, but that effort is always worth it. It keeps everyone, especially the leader, focused on the Big Picture and the Big Rocks.

Finally, if you want to ensure that:

1. Your performance management and expectations systems are being reviewed at least annually and
2. Team members are being given monthly, quarterly, and annual reviews of the performance level.

Those expectations must be written into the performance management and expectation systems for the *leaders* in your organization. You also need to devise, (if you haven't already done so) a system to track those Big Rock leader activities.

Expectations and your Selection Filter

To make sure your organization has a fair shot at sustaining operational excellence you want to make certain that the processes and filters you use to select team members are supporting that effort.

Much like performance management/expectations review systems, job descriptions are often created and then seldom revisited. I personally believe that this, in part, has given rise to the use of the phrase "and all other duties as assigned" in so many job descriptions. As a result, those persons tasked with recruiting interviewing and selecting new team members for your organization will have their ability to effectively do so diminished.

Remember that sometimes people aren't doing what we want them to do because what we want them to do is not a good fit for his or her skill set or temperament.

It's unrealistic to believe that there is such a thing as a perfect hiring or selection filter. But it's important to make sure that the criteria using to evaluate and select new team members is helping and not hindering your overall mission.

How will you know if your selection filter needs to be revisited?

Here's a simple way to tell:

If one or even 2 out of every 10 choices you made in selecting new team members or selecting a current team member for a new role didn't work out, you can chalk that up to the law of averages. It happens.

If however, you're missing 3 out of 10 times or more, your selection filter is working against you, not for you.

What steps can you take to make sure your selection or hiring filter is best serving your organization?

Consider doing the following:

1. Regularly revisit your performance management/expectation systems for the position you're hiring or selecting for.
2. Translate that performance management expectation system into a job description for the role in question.
3. Clearly identify the skills and temperament necessary to optimally execute the role.
4. Make that skill set and temperament a baseline requirement for selection.
5. If you want to consider potential as well, do some thorough research on the person's past work experience taking special note to evaluate his or her tendencies toward initiative and self-development and work ethic.

If the interviewer is not the leader that will be taking the person onto their team (in other words they may be an HR employee, recruitment firm, a scout, etc.), the interviewer should make sure to consult with the leader throughout the process and consider the leader as the final interviewer.

CHAPTER 6

WHAT GETS MEASURED, GETS DONE

A long held adage in the world of effectiveness is "what gets measured, gets done."

If we embrace that there is truth in this, then it follows that any organization that wants to maintain a consistently high level of effectiveness needs to be able to use metrics to monitor performance. More specifically, every one of your team's "Big Rocks" need to have quantifiable measurements associated with them. This can, however, be easier said than done.

There are some activities that lend themselves to being more quantifiable. Areas like sales, manufacturing, production levels, free throw percentages, call handling times and grade point averages are custom built to be easily countable and tabulated. Many organizations, however, also have important areas of focus (Big Rocks) that present more of a challenge when it comes to metrics.

Areas like customer satisfaction, employee morale, corporate reputation, while important are not as easily quantified. They require a more involved set or combination of metrics to meaningfully be measured. In other words, these areas require more time, work, and finesse to create meaningful metrics.

What often happens in organizations is that the more easily quantified Big Rocks activities garner more emphasis and attention. If the organization is unable or unwilling to create meaningful metrics for the seemingly more "intangible" Big Rocks, overall effectiveness in these areas may begin to suffer.

Interestingly, it is also not uncommon for the more easily attained metrics to be force fit to measure more intangible areas. Because metrics are (or should) be the primary determining factor in the distribution of carrots (rewards/recognition) and sticks (consequences), this can result in the inadvertent reward of inappropriate behavior and/or punishment of desirable behavior. Here are a couple of examples:

In a call center, one of the primary metrics managers monitor is the number of calls answered vs. those abandoned (customer hangs up rather than wait). It seems on the surface to make sense that you should reward the customer service representatives (CSR's) who take the most calls. The idea being their effort translates into fewer abandoned calls and fewer frustrated customers. Since calls answered per CSR in a call center is data that is relatively easy to gather, it would be pretty easy to see which CSR took the most calls over any given period of time.

Here's the complication: In a call center, customer service and satisfaction are also "Big Rocks". If you reward CSR's for taking the most calls you could be at the same time be encouraging, and even rewarding poor customer service behaviors. Being short with customers, not doing thorough enough analysis of customer issues, and even hanging up on customers are all behaviors that will help the "stats" of a CSR in the area of number of calls taken. They are also behaviors that can negatively impact customer satisfaction and retention.

Simply put it's important to make sure that metrics intended for one purpose do not inadvertently end up being used for another purpose. Here's an example of how easily that can happen.

In the call center where I worked we began to experience a substantial increase in call volume. It became clear that we needed to add staff to appropriately handle the increase. But there was a catch. You see, the folks in the Finance and HR departments understandably wanted to know that we were hiring (adding expense) in a way that was reflective of our needs (handling increased call volume). There would not be (and should not have been) a blank check to hire additional employees based on our "best guesses."

What was needed was a more scientific approach to justify hiring additional CSR's. We decided to hire a firm to do a "time & motion" study of our customer service department. The firm's job was to do a large sample study of the calls coming in to the center to determine the average call length. And so a team of individuals with stopwatches and clipboards set about the task of tracking the length of thousands of calls coming into our call center.

After an extensive study was completed it was determined that the average length of an incoming call was 240 seconds or four minutes. With that information we could now more accurately assess our staffing needs relative to our increased call volume. X number of calls per month at 240 seconds each equals Y number of staff required to handle those calls at an acceptable rate.

Now center management, Finance, and HR all had a working model to justify staffing levels. It's important to remember that this new metric had, initially as its sole purpose to be a tool to determine staffing levels. Strangely, within mere months, the metric for determining staffing levels (240 seconds per call) morphed into a performance standard for the CSR's. All of a sudden, it seemed, CSR's were now being evaluated in part based on whether they were handling calls within an average of a 240 second window of time.

It was an easy performance metric to put in place, as the data necessary to track it was easily accessible down to the individual CSR level. Individual call statistics by CSR were even available. Soon the CSR's were being critiqued on their average call handling time. If it was less than 240 seconds they received kudos on their stat sheets each day. If average call handling time was above 240 seconds the CSR was more likely to have that stat "highlighted" as an area of improvement.

It wasn't long before digital timers and stopwatches began to show up on CSR's desks. Even the training department got in on the act by reinforcing the "240 second rule" for new employees while they were still in training. CSR's now keenly aware of the "carrot and stick" approach associated with the 240 second rule began adapting their behaviors accordingly.

As the timers approached the 240-second mark, you could hear CSR's begin to wrap up their conversations with customers no matter where they actually were in the call resolution process. Customer's were now even being told "I'll call you right back to get this all wrapped up" because there was not yet a carrot/stick element associated to *outbound* calls.

What had been solely a metric for determining staffing needs had morphed into something completely different. You'll recall, by the way, that the time and motion study was just that. The study did not have a call quality component, and that was totally OK as long as its use did not spill over into the realm of CSR management.

But it did. As a result, call length began informally to trump call quality in the minds of the person we'd entrusted to deliver world-class customer service. Quantity became ultimately more important than quality.

If you're wondering why I've included this lengthy example in this discourse on metrics, consider this. The company that went through this experience was not some prehistoric, archaic, stuck in the mud company. In my opinion, it was one of the most forward thinking and innovative organizations I've ever had the honor to work for. If it can happen in an organization with that kind of pedigree, it can happen in your organization, too.

This scenario makes it even more clear that what gets measured gets done, even if it's to the greater detriment of the organization.

So what's the solution?

When you develop "Big Rock" metrics for your organization, keep the following in mind.

1. When you develop (or review) the "Big Rock" metrics for your organization make sure that those metrics aren't in conflict with one another.

2. Consider using multiple metrics in coordination with each other to help you with recognition efforts. For example, CSR recognition (in our example) would be better in alignment with organizational goals if it were based on a blend of efficiency (calls handled) and quality (quality assurance monitoring scores).

3. Build meaningful metrics into your formal and informal performance review systems.

4. Make meaningful metrics easily accessible. When team members have visibility to metrics that they are being measured by, they are more empowered to monitor, manage and take ownership of their own performance.

5. Make it a "Big Rock" to continually look for ways to refine the metrics your organization relies on to measure operational effectiveness.

Include utilization of "The 20 Foot Rule" as part of this ongoing refinement process. While, as the old cliché goes "numbers don't lie," they can cloud the issue if you're not careful. Make sure that your metrics are sound because what's measured gets done; for better or for worse.

CHAPTER 7

MEANINGFUL RECOGNITION

Earlier in the book, we identified Leadership Reality Check #7 as 'People need to feel recognized and appreciated for good performance'. In addition to providing feedback, which we'll discuss at length later in the book, the other prescribed strategy was to create a meaningful recognition program – with emphasis on the word *meaningful*.

Some might say that any recognition program is better than no recognition program at all. That is probably true. But to help you and your organization sustain optimal performance and operational excellence over the long term it is critical that your recognition programs be perceived as meaningful to those who are being recognized.

The consequences to recognition that is not perceived to be meaningful, as we discussed earlier in the book are:

1. The recipients of the recognition could end up feeling slighted or unappreciated.
2. The giver of the recognition could end up feeling that the recipients are being unappreciative and ungrateful.

So what can you as a leader do to make sure recognition in your organization is meaningful?

I submit that there are 9 things to take a serious look at. They are listed here in no certain order, except for the 1st one.

1. Actually have a recognition program.
I know. It seems a bit obvious. But if the only recognition your organization boasts is giving out a paycheck you could be in deep trouble. If your organization is volunteer-based you can't even claim the paycheck as recognition. Making a definitive move in your organization to create some type of structured recognition program in and of itself will signal to your team that you feel that it is important. Your team will be at least nominally convinced that you get it. They'll also probably be thinking it's about time!

2. Make it meaningful by explaining it clearly.
Albert Einstein was quoted as saying "If you can't explain it simply, you don't understand it well enough". This quote is relevant when it comes to your recognition program and how you roll it out to your organization. If your recognition program is perceived to be arduous, complex and boring it will likely be dead on arrival with your team.

Too much complexity can also leave your team suspicious of the program's intent and/or value. When someone receives recognition from such a program, while they might like the reward in the short term, this can still be a problematic situation. Why? Because, if they aren't clear as to how and why they were recognized, it is difficult for them to know how or which behaviors to repeat to garner such recognition again in the future.

Remember, we are looking for sustained optimal performance. If recipients of recognition don't know how they got the recognition, sustaining the rewarded behavior becomes difficult. Especially if they aren't sure exactly what the rewarded behavior is.

I was once asked to speak at a kickoff meeting for a nationally known organization. One of the people in attendance suddenly saw his name flash on the screen as employee of the year. As he got up to the stage to receive his reward and was asked to say a few words here's what he said:

"I'm not sure how I got this, but I'll take it. Thanks!"

After an awkward silence, the obligatory applause from the audience began and as the employee of the year made it back to his seat he could be seen acknowledging words of congratulations with a shrug of the shoulders.

I was left thinking, "He really has no idea why he's employee of the year". Further, the people in the audience were left with little or no idea as to how they might receive such recognition in the future.

Let me be clear. I'm not implying that there wasn't ample reason for this fellow to receive such high praise. To the contrary, I'm sure there were numerous significant reasons for his receiving this great honor. But if he and the organization at large aren't clear on what the criteria was that moved him to the front of the pack, the impact of the recognition will most assuredly be short-term.

Your recognition program and the criteria that support it must be easily and widely understood to maximize and sustain its impact and meaningfulness.

3. Recognition tends to be more meaningful when it is based upon credible data.

When team members have some faith in the reliability of the data being used for recognition, the recognition program gets greater buy-in from the team.

Depending upon the level of sophistication of your performance reporting systems, this can be a bigger challenge for some organizations than for others. Data that is compiled from automated tracking systems is ideal in that the need for human intervention to compile the data is significantly reduced. In other words, data compiled with computer-generated sales report will likely be seen as more credible than tabulations made by manual tick sheets produced by the individuals vying for the recognition.

It's not that your team members are less than virtuous. It's more that when Person A and Person B are in the running for recognition, and the results are based on data they manually produced themselves, the credibility of the data and the resulting recognition can become suspect.

Similarly, there may be recognition that is principally based on subjective criteria. (Example: An award for best team spirit.). Even in situations like this, there should be a clearly defined idea as to what the criteria is for such recognition. If the recognition criteria lacks clarity, the meaningfulness of the recognition will suffer.

4. Meaningful recognition relies on readily accessible data.

In addition to having the recognition be understandable and based on credible data, it is important that the data being used is easily accessible to potential recipients of the recognition.

As obvious as this seems, I've seen numerous situations where say the data being used for quarterly contest only comes out once a month. That isn't horrible, but it only gives the competing teams an opportunity to see where they are in the running two times over the course of 90 days before the recognition is awarded at the end of the 3rd month. In scenarios like this, multiple opportunities for course correction or picking up the pace (when you know you're behind) are lost. The result often is a feeling on the part of team members of "If we had known we were this close (or far behind) we could have made an extra push". In most of these types of cases, it wasn't that information wasn't available. It was that it was only shared with the affected parties once a month.

Even worse, there are some situations I've seen where those competing for the recognition didn't received any information as to where they stood in relation to other potential recipients until the recognition was actually given. As a result all affected parties thought they were leading the pack. In reality, most were far behind the leaders and never knew it until "Awards Night".

If you want your team to perform optimally over a sustained period of time and recognition is one of your strategies for making that happen, err on the side of providing too much data than too little. It will give your team more of an opportunity to manage their own performance.

5. Recognition is more meaningful when you strike the proper balance between MVP and Incentive-based recognition programs.
Most recognition is based on 2 types of reward systems:

1.   MVP-based recognition
2.   Incentive-based recognition

It's very important that your organization's recognition strategy reflects a balance of each of these approaches. Let's define each of these types of recognition and then discuss why striking a balance between them is important.

MVP-based recognition usually focuses on the best of the best in a particular performance area. Awards for "top salesperson", "top scorer", and "top fundraiser" are examples of MVP-based recognition. Recognizing your top performers is critical to effective recognition because it heralds the efforts of the team member who had the most significant individual impact on a particular key area of your operation. If however all your recognition strategies are all MVP-based they could be putting a damper on efforts of the other team members.

For example, in many organizations the MVP in a certain area stands head and shoulders above the next closest performers. If this is the case, the other team members can begin to think that "We'll never catch him or her, so what's the use in trying?" So even while your MVP continues to strive and thrive, the performance of the other team members can begin to wane.

Incentive-based recognition centers on rewarding team members that reach a certain level of accomplishment or achievement. Let's say that your average widget sales per team member stands at 6 widgets per day. You may create incentive-based recognition where all team members that sell at least 10 widgets today will experience a reward of some type. While this incentive-based recognition can potentially provide rewards for every team member, it's important that all your recognition strategies not be incentive-based. Here's why.

You may be driving a higher level of performance for your team at-large, but if you have a team member that sells 35 widgets today and the recognition for that level of performance is the same as for the team members that sell 10 widgets per day, it could cause some issues.

Your 35 widgets per day MVP performer will not see any justification (as it relates to recognition) for their putting in the additional effort. So while you may get an uptick in performance from the team in general, reduced effort and production from your MVP performer could cancel out those gains.

The solution I'm recommending here is that your recognition strategy for your team strike a balance of MVP based and incentive based recognition. Striking a balance will create an atmosphere where you can drive performance from every member of your team.

6. Meaningful recognition is connected to your "Big Rocks"

Tying your recognition efforts to your organizational "Big Rocks" has multiple benefits.

1. You are using recognition to focus and enhance performance that impacts those aspects of your organization that are most important.
2. You are reinforcing in the minds of your team members what the priorities are for the organization.
3. In so doing, you're creating an environment where your team members make better decisions relative to your organizational priorities.

How do you make Big Rock connections to your recognition efforts?

Prominently and regularly use the name of the Big Rock that is being targeted and impacted by the recognition

For example:

"One of our company's primary areas of focus is to create a **great customer experience (Big Rock)**. The employees we are recognizing today demonstrated by their example what customer service excellence looks like".

"**Community outreach (Big Rock)** is one of the cornerstones of our organization. The volunteers we recognize today stand as a glowing example of what it looks like to give your time and talent beyond the walls of our day-to-day jobs and make a difference in the lives of others. "

Big Rock language is powerful and should be a mainstay in the development and execution of your recognition strategies. You should even consider adding Big Rock language to certificates, plaques, trophies, and other tangible representations of your recognition.

When you administer recognition it should be easy for recipients and others to "get it" when it comes to understand how recognizing performance connects to your organizational Big Rocks.

7. Make sure you are recognizing the right behaviors.
In the Metrics chapter, we discussed how easily metrics could be misused as a performance management tool. The same goes for recognition.

For example, you may wish to recognize employee that ask for the most referrals, but if no one ever follows up on referrals, they haven't really benefited your organization.

Similarly, if you wish to recognize the coach who recruits the best scorers amongst high school candidates, but those individuals have not also shown that they have the skills necessary to succeed academically, their contribution to your team will be short term at best. In effect, you will be rewarding coaches for creating a revolving door of players in the organization.

The moral to the story here is that except in a few cases, basing your recognition on a single metric can produce results that ultimately could be a detriment to your organization. A good rule of thumb is to use multiple factors to shape your recognition. Creating a formula from a blend of metrics for recognition is usually more effective in driving the performance you're looking for.

For example, in the case of recognition for referrals, you may wish to recognize the person who generated the highest number of referrals that resulted in *sales*.

8. *Meaningful recognition employs the "20 Foot Rule"*
Remember the elevator speech from Van Uere's 20 Foot Rule?

One of the key benefits to engaging the people you want to recognize in the creation of the recognition program is that their involvement translates into greater buy-in and ownership of the program. There are a couple of ways to engage your team in creating meaningful recognition programs.

Use the 20 Foot Rule to Creatively name/brand your recognition program
Recognition is more meaningful when it's fun. One of the ways to make it more fun right out of the gate is to creatively brand the program. Encourage your team members to use themes

around sports teams, popular movies, etc. , to add spice to the program. You'll be surprised how your team will take an idea and run with it. While this adds fun to the program, it also allows your team members to more personally identify themselves with the program.

Using the 20 Foot Rule to identify what prizes will be
Many leaders are hesitant to engage their teams in determining what the prize(s) will be for the recognition. This is usually because the leader assumes that their team members will ask for the universe. Often, the unfortunate outcome of this miscalculation on the part of the leader results in the distribution of "socket sets" as prizes.

To help assuage this concern, you as the leader can identify what resources will be available for the recognition. You can also set parameters such as making sure there is a balance between MVP and Incentive-based recognition. You will likely find, as have many leaders that have tried this before, that this approach can really add value to your recognition.

For example, one business owner I met wanted to do a sales contest for her employees. Rather than tell them what the prize would be for the winner, she told him what the dollar value of the prize would be. After letting her team work through a discussion of what the prize would be for the winner of the contest, she was pleasantly surprised by their solution.

It turned out that they could not agree on what the prize should be for the sales contest. But because the owner identified that $150 would be used to fund the prize, they came up with an innovative solution.

Each employee identified what he or she would like the $150 to go towards if they won a contest.

Here's how it worked out:

- Employee #1: Wanted cash
- Employee #2: Was a chocoholic and wanted a gift certificate to the Chocolatier Shop in town
- Employee #3: Wanted a gift certificate to a local spa
- Employee #4: Wanted time off from work to allow him to see his daughter's high school softball games, which usually started before he got off work.

Every employee was now working to win a contest whose prize really meant something to him or her personally.

Simply put, to make your recognition more meaningful consider engaging the potential recipients in creating the program. You should still own program parameters, determine the specific performance you want to drive, and the resources you want to dedicate toward the prize. But where you can, you should make an effort to engage your team in other aspects of the program, take and make the most of that opportunity.

9. Make it meaningful by making it timely.
One of the more simple yet powerful ways to make your recognition more meaningful is to make it timely. When someone earns recognition of any type, the perceived value of the recognition is increased if it is delivered right away.

In other words, if I win a sales contest that has as a prize of a $100 gift card but I have to wait 10 days to 2 weeks to receive it, the impact of that recognition is diminished. I'll still be happy about the prize, but having to wait for it will take some of the joy of winning it away. It also won't make much sense to me. Especially since I, as the contest winner and the rest of the team will probably be thinking "Didn't you know when the announcement of the contest winner was going to be? Then why weren't you prepared?"

Publilius Syrus, a Latin writer of mimes in the 1st century B. C. , known for his aphorisms on life captured the point I'm trying to make very well when he wrote. "He who gives promptly, gives twice."

In summary, recognition that is timely is recognition that is meaningful.

How much should you spend on recognition?

I'm no expert on determining what the optimum amount is that you should invest in recognition. In the most basic sense however, here's my 2 cents (pun intended).

The activities and behaviors that you are recognizing should have some fiscal impact on your organization. In other words, those activities should result in increased revenue, reduced expenses, or both.

It seems to me that it follows that your starting place would be to quantify what those fiscal impacts are in real dollars and cents (or whatever currency you trade in). From there, your determination as to what % of those fiscal impacts you should allocate to your recognition programs is really up to you. The key is to make sure that the determination of your recognition budget is a data driven decision.

I can report though, that what I hear from many leaders is that when their people know the fiscal impact of their behavior and they (the leader) err on the side of generosity with their recognition, the results are very positive. These leaders report more consistent and sustained desirable behaviors. And that's the whole point, right?

CHAPTER 8

DELIVERING EFFECTIVE FEEDBACK

Many of the suggested strategies for sustaining operational excellence discussed so far in this book relate to feedback. In my seminars, as a way of initiating dialog around the subject of feedback, I typically ask the group a battery of questions regarding feedback and its value as a leadership/management tool.

The exchange with the audience usually goes something like this:

Me: "Is feedback critical to the success of an organization?"

Audience:"Yes"

Me: "Can it be one of the most powerful tools at a leaders disposal?"

Audience: "Yes"

Me: "Is it also cost effective?"

Audience: "Yes"

Me:"Do we provide feedback as often as we should?"

Audience: "No"

After getting the "no" response to the last question around whether we provide feedback as much as we should, I pause with a somewhat perplexed look on my face and then I repeat the same battery of questions, as if I missed something the first time around.

I always get the same responses when I repeat the questions. It's clear that everyone in the room feels the same disconnect between value and execution when it comes to feedback.

The real question becomes "If we know feedback is possibly the most critical, powerful, cost effective tool in the leaders toolbox, why don't we provide it as often as we should?"

The reasons provided by audience members probably won't surprise you much. They may reflect your reasons as well. Here are some of the reasons people typically offer.

They don't know how to do it
They know intuitively that it's important but have never been taught how to deliver feedback effectively and efficiently. In other words, for some it's a "skill" issue.

Conflict avoidance
They don't want to deal with the confrontation that could arise from giving feedback. Instead, they enter conflict avoidance mode. Often this is justified by saying things like: "It wasn't that big a deal", "It probably was a one time thing", "I don't want to make a bad situation worse", etc.

Interestingly, the reason for not giving feedback seems to assume that feedback is always or mostly about addressing problematic behaviors.

It's unnecessary
In this case the belief is that the person already knows the "error of their ways". To make mention of the obvious by providing feedback would just amount to piling on or stating the obvious.

I don't get feedback
As unusual as it seems, there are people who take the position that since they don't get feedback, they aren't going to provide it to anyone else. This isn't always as juvenile as it may seem on the surface.

In some cases, what the person is inferring is that they aren't sure how well *they* are doing and by extension may not be comfortable giving feedback to others. Or as is the case for many of us that had our own stint with "Pathetica", we may not have had a positive example to follow from our early days as an employee.

Not enough time
Without question the most common reason given by people I've spoken to for not giving as much feedback as they should is that they simply don't have the time. Between meetings, putting out "fires", writing reports, etc. , there just isn't enough time to have meaningful conversations with team members around their performance.

None of these reasons for not giving enough feedback are fictional or contrived. They reflect the very real world that leaders operate in every day. That being said, if meaningful feedback isn't delivered effectively, efficiently, and regularly it can signal the beginning of the end of sustained operational excellence in your organization.

Feedback gives the leader the ability to course correct behaviors that have become out of synch with organizational objectives. Feedback also provides incentive to team members to sustain desirable behaviors.

So how, you ask, can we make sure that feedback is an integral part of every leaders job? I submit that it will require the shifting of some paradigms and some blueprints for execution. Let's start with the paradigm shifts.

Feedback Paradigm Shift
Treat Feedback as a BIG ROCK

If you remember from earlier in the book the conversation about Big Rocks (priorities) you'll recall that the key to getting important things done is to put the "Big Rocks" in the jar first.

With regards to feedback that means it will be necessary to position feedback as something that not only should take place, but must take place consistently in your organization. It can no longer be seen as something you'll do if you have time for it. In concrete terms that means that feedback needs to take precedence over endless/numerous meetings for example. Also, I think a case can be ably made that most of the "fire (crisis) fighting" that leaders find themselves doing could have been headed off at the pass by proactively addressing issues rather than reactively addressing them.

Consider this. If you are a leader in an organization that does annual performance or merit reviews, is feedback and coaching reflected as a Big Rock among the items *you* are being held accountable for? Or is it, as it is for many, more of a back page performance/merit review category (i. e. "smaller rock")?

If leaders knew that their performance reviews would be heavily impacted (i. e. impact possible increase in compensation) by the emphasis they have placed on giving employees/team members feedback, I can almost guarantee you that feedback would run rampant. Now don't get me wrong. I don't think that the only way to get leaders to focus more energy and time on feedback is to impact their wallet. But for some, it will.

Making the delivery of feedback a "Big Rock" for your leadership team would, in effect, create a reward/consequence (carrot/stick) system around the activity of feedback in your organization.

To sum it up, if you want feedback to be a staple in your organization, a great first step would be to make feedback a tangible "Big Rock" for the persons who serve in leadership roles in your organization.

Feedback Paradigm Shift
Terms for Feedback Redefined

I'm editorializing a bit here, but I believe that one of the other major stumbling blocks with feedback is in part the terms we've come to associate with it; namely *positive* feedback and *negative* feedback. When I ask audience members to define these terms, I consistently get the following response:

Positive feedback is feedback you give when something you like happens. Negative feedback is feedback you give when something you don't like happens. This definition of negative feedback in a way implies that when you give it, the result will be a negative experience (confrontational, defensive, etc.).

In an attempt to more accurately characterize feedback from the *recipient's* perspective I believe that a redefinition of these terms is in order.

Try these redefinitions on for size:

Positive feedback (redefined) is feedback that works.

Negative feedback (redefined) is feedback that does not work.

Here's where I'm going with all this. It's possible that an attempt to deliver "positive feedback" (original definition) could be met with contempt. An example would be the leader who constantly exclaims "Great Job!" or "Good Work!" without ever saying what's great about the job or good about the work in question. If this behavior by the leader becomes "habitual" it can leave the team member with the impression that the comments ring hollow ("What's great about it?" "Does he/she even know what I do?").

In this instance, attempts at positive feedback (original definition) could begin to come across as shallow cheerleading. This is certainly not the worst thing in the world, but without more substantive information, the team member may not be sure about what exactly it is they are doing that they should continue doing.

Ultimately, the result could be that attempts at positive feedback (original definition) could end up being negative feedback (redefined as feedback that doesn't work). The whole point of feedback is to help team members consistently move the organization forward in the execution of its mission.

So what's the solution?

I submit that we should engage new terms around feedback. Terms that more accurately represent what it is that feedback should be helping to accomplish.

Feedback Paradigm Shift
New Terms for a New Paradigm

Rather than using the term positive and negative for feedback, I suggest that we use terms that paint a clearer picture as to what feedback is really suppose to accomplish. We'll start by asking you to replace the phrase "positive" feedback with *Feedback to Reinforce.*

Feedback to Reinforce more accurately gets at what this type of feedback is all about. To define it more specifically, Feedback to Reinforce is feedback you deliver when you observe a behavior that you want to see repeated given the same or similar circumstances. The point of Feedback to Reinforce is that it is designed to sustain desired behaviors. This should also be the goal that leader has as he or she works toward sustaining operational excellence in the organization.

Similarly, rather than use the term "negative" feedback I suggest that you use the term *Feedback to Develop.* We'll define Feedback to Develop as feedback you deliver when you observe a behavior that you'd like to see altered or replaced given the same or similar circumstances. Feedback to Develop then is designed to offer a course correction for behaviors that are not in alignment with your organizational goals or mission.

I'm suggesting using the terms Feedback to Reinforce and Feedback to Develop because neither term inherently signals a "negative" conversation.

Reinforcement and Development are at the core of what effective leaders do (or should be doing) consistently. And given the fact we know that feedback is requisite strategy for dealing with a number of reasons why people aren't doing what we need them to do, these new terms for a new paradigm position you well as you seek to sustain operational excellence in your organization.

To maximize the effectiveness of your feedback however, it is important that when delivered it consistently contains some critical components.

FEEDBACK
4 Critical Components

Now that we've begun the process of shifting the paradigms around feedback by introducing new terms, it's time to start offering some architecture to the feedback process. We'll start that effort by identifying the 4 critical components that are part of all effective feedback conversations.

These critical components are:

1. Clear expectations
2. Context
3. Specificity
4. Impact

Let's discuss each of these components in more detail to describe why they are key to the delivery of effective feedback.

Clear Expectations
This component of feedback actually takes place before the feedback is even given.

If the point of feedback is to offer reinforcement and/or development for team members it should be clear that as a prerequisite, the person receiving the feedback should already clearly know what it is that you expect of them. Feedback that is given without the pre-existence of clearly communicated expectations isn't really feedback; it is "notification".

There is a classic signal that feedback wasn't preceded by clearly communicated expectations. It is usually heard when a team member, after having a conversation (feedback) about his or her behavior responds by saying, "No one ever told me that!" Simply put, for feedback of any type to reach maximum effectiveness, it should be preceded by clearly communicated expectations. I can assure you that feedback conversations that aren't preceded by clearly communicated expectations will more often than not be perceived as "negative". It leaves the team member feeling as though they are being held accountable for something that they are not aware of.

Context

Context is about 2 things really.

First it's about framing the conversation up front so that the person receiving the feedback has some idea about what you're talking about. If you've ever found yourself in the middle of a conversation before you really figured out what the person really came to talk to you about, you'll understand exactly the point I'm making here.

Feedback should never feel to the recipient like it's being embedded in another conversation or worse, feel like it's coming out of nowhere. Later in this chapter we'll show you how to simply and effectively frame your feedback conversation.

Secondly, with regard to feedback, we use the term context to drive home the point that the feedback being given should be delivered as close in time as possible to the observed behavior. The more time there is between the observed behavior(s) and the feedback on those behaviors, the less effective the feedback is likely to be. As time passes the feedback recipient's recollection of the event may begin to fade. Further, similar activities may have taken place since the initial behavior for which you wanted to provide (or should have provided) feedback. Those similar activities would also likely have benefitted from your timely feedback.

Making feedback timely exponentially increases the effectiveness and overall impact of your feedback. Translation: making feedback timely should be a "Big Rock" for any leader with direct reports.

Specificity

Specificity is all about making sure that during your feedback sessions you discuss specific, *observable behaviors.*

In the case of "Feedback to Reinforce" this will give the recipient of the feedback something tangible to focus on as they seek to repeat or recreate desired behaviors. In the case of "Feedback to Develop" focusing on specific behaviors can provide similar clarity with regard to behaviors that need to be avoided or altered in some way.

You may have noticed the emphasis here on the terms *observable* and *behavior.* That's no accident. Feedback is most effective when it focuses on things seen or witnessed by the deliverer of the feedback. The more persons removed from the actual observation of the behavior the feedback giver is (i. e. feedback based on behaviors witnessed by others), the more diminished the feedback's effectiveness will be.

This doesn't mean that feedback should only be limited to what the leader personally witnesses, it's just a statement of fact. To counteract this, make sure that feedback you are giving on events that you don't personally observe (someone's behavior with a customer, in a meeting, or in an email exchange, for example) is as specific and detailed as you can make it. Doing so will help your credibility in the conversation and make the feedback feel more professional and less personal.

You may also have noticed that there has been no mention of the term *attitude*. That's because addressing attitude in a feedback session is one of the biggest traps that leaders fall prey to. For example, let's say you want to give someone Feedback to Reinforce on his or her great attitude. First of all, how do *you* know what kind of attitude they have? It could be that they've had a horrible day with lots of personal issues weighing on them. In other words, unless you have the gift of reading minds, you really don't know what kind of attitude they have. And by the way, their *attitude* is really none of your concern.

What you can speak to however, is what behaviors they are exhibiting. When we perceive someone to have a good attitude it's because they are exhibiting behaviors that we associate with a good attitude. For example, they smile, make eye contact, focus on solutions vs. problems, interact well with teammates, etc. Similarly, people whom we perceive to have bad attitudes demonstrate a completely different set of behaviors. They may roll their eyes frequently in meetings, shift blame for issues to others, rarely smile or more likely frown often, and focus on problems vs. solutions.

When you feel compelled to give someone feedback on their attitude, focus instead on the behaviors they are putting on display that are influencing your coming to that conclusion.

Impact
Impact in feedback is all about what happened or could happen as a result of a particular behavior or group of behaviors.

It's the part of feedback that highlights the theory of cause and effect; of action and reaction. When the impact of a behavior is part of feedback it signals not just what to do (or not do), but why. You may recall that earlier in the book we discussed that one of the reasons that people aren't doing what we want or need them to do is because they don't know why they should do it.

A well constructed impact statement, as part of your feedback will help you address the "why" question for the recipient. When people understand why they should or should not be doing something, that insight can provide them with their own energy or motivation to stay on track.

Addressing the "why" question through an impact statement also does something else very important. It acknowledges your appreciation for the fact that this person is indeed capable of being a thinking person. Gone are the days of "because I said so" for those in leadership positions. Unless of course sustained operational excellence is unimportant to you.

Interestingly, impact statements are often found absent in feedback discussions for an interesting reason. The person giving the feedback often assumes that since *they* know why something is important, that the recipient should know why it's important as well. One gentleman in one of my classes said it in a more interesting way. "It should be obvious!" Perhaps. But because the impact of a behavior should be obvious, it may not always be. In fact, because there are often multiple impacts for any given behavior, the recipient of the feedback may be aware of some of those impacts, but not all of them.

For example, someone may understand inherently that when they are absent from work that it impacts the leaders impression of that person's reliability. The person may not however, realize how their absence impacts workload distribution, customer wait times, organizational productivity, etc.

Summary

So now we've not only communicated that feedback should be a priority ("Big Rock") for all leaders, we've also suggested new terms for feedback, and to top it all off we've suggested that all effective feedback has 4 critical components.

- Clear expectations
- Context
- Specificity
- Impact

Right about now you may be thinking, "what about '*I don't have enough time for all this*' is this guy missing?" Point well taken. But what if I could give you a model for delivering feedback that embraces the new paradigm, and allows for you to set the proper context for the feedback, identify and discuss specific behaviors, and speak to the impact (or multiple impacts) of said behaviors, all in 2 minutes or less (which is, by the way probably less time than you spend thinking or obsessing about the behavior in question).

Would you be interested?

Read on!

Delivering Effective Feedback in 2 Minutes or Less
Feedback to Reinforce

Now let's spend some time getting down to practical steps for delivering feedback effectively and efficiently. What we'll provide here is a model or "footprints on the dance floor" approach. The goal is to make sure we can efficiently deliver Feedback to Reinforce and Feedback to Develop in a way that incorporates all the critical components we discussed earlier.

We'll accomplish this by using some simple "sentence starters". Let's begin with Feedback to Reinforce.

Feedback to Reinforce Model

To deliver Feedback to Reinforce we'll use 4 "sentence starters".

1. "I'd like to speak with you about…"
2. "I like or I appreciate…"
3. "That's important because…"
4. "Thank you for…"

Each of these sentence starters has a specific role.

The first sentence starter: **"I'd like to speak with you about…"** helps you provide context for the feedback by identifying in general terms what you're discussing and when it took place.

The second sentence starter: **"I like/appreciate…"** is where you will provide specific details about the behavior in question. Starting this sentence with "I like" or "I appreciate" sends an early signal that this feedback is for behavior that you find desirable.

The third sentence starter, **"That's important because…"** let's you identify the impact(s) of the behavior(s) in question. You can spotlight how the behavior positively impacted your team, your clients, your productivity, and even your relationship with that particular team member.

You don't have to overdo it by discussing every possible impact. Instead, choose to highlight those areas of impact that the person may not be aware of and/or those that are most substantive.

The fourth sentence starter: **"Thank you for…"** gives you the opportunity to reinforce the behavior with an expression of gratitude and a note of encouragement to "keep up the good work".

So, to summarize, the 4 sentence starters for Feedback to Reinforce are:

1. "I'd like to speak with you about…"(Context)
2. "I like/appreciate…"(Specificity)
3. "That's important because…"(Impact)
4. "Thank you for…"(Appreciation/Reinforcement)

Now that we have a model to operate by, let's see how it might play out using a sample scenario.

Feedback to Reinforce
Sample Scenario

Let's say that earlier this morning, an employee followed through on providing you critical information for an escalated customer complaint you are handling. The customer is Ms. Brown and she's upset because she's asked for a copy of her bill 3 times and she still doesn't have it. She's asked to speak to the manager (you) and you've committed to get a copy emailed to her within the hour. In addition you promised her a follow-up call to make sure she is satisfied.

The only problem is that you're headed into a meeting with your boss's boss who's visiting your office today. You explain the situation to your employee (Greg) and task him with getting a copy of Ms. Brown's bill emailed to her. Greg does so in 30 minutes and even makes the follow-up call to Ms. Brown when he realizes that you'll probably be tied up longer than expected in your meeting.

This would be a classic example of a situation where you'd want to deliver "Feedback to Reinforce" to Greg. If this or a similar situation took place again, you'd definitely want Greg to respond in a similar manner.

Given this example, let's see how the Feedback to Reinforce model might be utilized.

1. **"Greg, I'd like to speak with you about** the situation you helped out on this morning with Ms. Brown. "(Context)
2. **"I really appreciate** how you not only got the invoice copy emailed to her, but also took the initiative to call her to

follow-up. Especially when you knew I might be delayed in doing so because of my meeting. "(Specificity)

3. "**That was really important because** we pride ourselves on being responsive to our customers, and while Ms. Brown up to this point may have lost some faith in us, you helped to restore it by acting efficiently and professionally in handling her request. It's also important and reassuring to know that when I give you an important task like this one, I can count on it being done. "(Impact)

4. "**Thank you for** following through and keep up the good work!" (Appreciation/Reinforcement)

Now that you've read through this use of the Feedback to Reinforce model, go back and read it aloud and see how long it took. Put that time here:_____

As you read through the Feedback to Reinforce model, I hope you took note of a couple of things.

First, in the 3rd step (impact) we actually identified not one, but two impacts from Greg's behavior.

1. He restored our customer's image of us as a responsive organization
2. He reinforced my belief that I can count on him to follow-up and follow through on important tasks.

One impact was company related. The other was trust/relationship related. Both are important.

The second thing I would have you notice is that the scenarios that are good candidates for Feedback to Reinforce don't have to be because the person saved your organization millions of dollars, ended hunger on the planet, or orchestrated world peace.

Any time someone in your organization does something that moves the organization's mission forward in a positive manner, no matter how big or small, it makes for a great opportunity to provide Feedback to Reinforce. In fact, a great argument could be made that reinforcing the small things helps to reinforce the big stuff.

Feedback to Reinforce
Practicum

Now it's your turn!

I'd like you to think of 3 instances in the past week where some-one in your professional or personal life has done something that would warrant you providing them with Feedback to Reinforce. Try to include at least one personal example.

You'll notice that I mentioned having you recall professional *and* personal examples. That's because the models we're providing work equally well for both. And truth be told, many of us are better at giving Feedback to Reinforce at work than we are at home. I believe that we all become better at this feedback thing when we take a more holistic approach to it.

What we'll do for each scenario is break down the context, specifics and impact(s) of the behaviors in question. Then we'll actually have you translate that information into the model for Feedback to Reinforce.

Finally, we'll get you to speak the feedback out loud and make a note of how long it took.

Real World Scenario # 1 for Feedback to Reinforce

Write down a brief answer to each of these questions

What was it about?

When did it take place?

What specific behaviors do you want altered/changed?

What was /were the impact(s) of the behavior(s)?

Now plug Real World Scenario #1 into the Feedback to Reinforce model.

Scenario # 1

1) _____(person's name), I'd like to speak with you a moment about:

2) I really like/appreciate:

3) That's important because:

4) Thank you for:

Now read the scenario out loud. How long did it take?

Real World Scenario # 2 for Feedback to Reinforce

Write down a brief answer to each of these questions

What was it about?

When did it take place?

What specific behaviors do you want altered/changed?

What was /were the impact(s) of the behavior(s)?

Now plug Real World Scenario # 2 into the Feedback to Reinforce model.

Scenario # 2

1) _____(person's name), I'd like to speak with you a moment about:

2) I really like/appreciate:

3) That's important because:

4) Thank you for:

Now read the scenario out loud. How long did it take?

Real World Scenario # 3 for Feedback to Reinforce

Write down a brief answer to each of these questions

What was it about?

When did it take place?

What specific behaviors do you want altered/changed?

What was /were the impact(s) of the behavior(s)?

Now plug Real World Scenario #3 into the Feedback to Reinforce model.

Scenario #3

1) _____(person's name), I'd like to speak with you a moment about:

2) I really like/appreciate:

3) That's important because:

4) Thank you for:

Now read the scenario out loud. How long did it take?

Additional Notes on Feedback to Reinforce

Using your own words?
You no doubt began to use your own wording for the sentence starters. That's fantastic! The point is not so much about following a rigid script. It's more about making sure you provide context, specificity, and impact in your feedback.

Bouncing around a bit?
You may also find that you bounced around a bit between specificity and impact (sentence starters 2 & 3). That's totally OK! It's not unusual during the course of conversation to bounce back and forth a bit. The key is to make sure you specifically identified the behaviors in question, when they took place, and what the impacts were for those behaviors during your feedback.

Does this seem a little one-sided?
You're probably noticing that this particular feedback model is designed principally as a one-way conversation, but it doesn't have to be. You may find, at times, that your Feedback to Reinforce opens other avenues for dialog. That's a good thing. The model, however, is principally designed for effectiveness and efficiency. You'll likely find that this efficient "stick and move" (boxing metaphor), approach will be appreciated by the recipients of your feedback. After all, they are busy people, too.

Why we used real world scenarios
Finally, since you identified 3 real world scenarios to plug into the Feedback to Reinforce model, I have a relatively important question for you: Did you actually have these conversations yet? If not, there is no time like the present (context).

Delivering Effective Feedback in 2 minutes or less
Feedback to Develop 1.0

Obviously, all the feedback you give won't be to reinforce behaviors. You will on occasion need to provide feedback in an effort to alter or replace a behavior. That's where Feedback to Develop 1.0 comes in.

From the 1.0 designation you've probably already correctly concluded that there is probably a Feedback to Develop 2.0 somewhere on the horizon. We'll look at that model a little later. For now, let's take a look at the model for delivering Feedback to Develop 1.0.

Feedback to Develop 1.0 – The Model

Just as we did with Feedback to Reinforce we'll be using "sentence starters" to guide the feedback discussion. Rather than 4 sentence starters, the Feedback to Develop 1.0 model will incorporate the use of 7 sentence starters. Here they are:

1. "I'd like to speak with you about…"
2. "I noticed…"
3. "What that means is…"
4. "What I need instead is…"
5. "What suggestions do you have…"
6. "Good'. What that will do is…"
7. "Can I count on you to…?"

Let's look at the important role each of these sentence starters plays.

The first sentence starter for Feedback to Develop 1.0, **"I'd like to speak with you about…"** is designed to set the context of the feedback. It should look familiar, as it is also the first sentence starter for Feedback to Reinforce. That is absolutely intentional.

The reason you'd want to consistently open your feedback discussions, whether they are to reinforce or to develop, with similar phrasing is so that you won't unwittingly divulge what kind of feedback you're about to deliver. If you always begin your feedback with the same basic words, the recipient of your feedback will be less likely to anticipate the nature of your conversation.

If you tend to start feedback to develop with a different phrase or disposition, the recipient may begin to brace himself or herself and/or put up shields as a defensive posture before you even tell them why you're there. This could seriously impair the person's ability or willingness to listen clearly to what you have to say.

The second sentence starter, **"I noticed…"** is where you will detail the specific behaviors(s) in question. You'll notice that this sentence starter is **"I noticed…"** vs. **"I like/appreciate…"** from Feedback to Reinforce. That's because you probably don't "like/appreciate" the behavior you're discussing. The phrase "I noticed…" signals a different tone, but it is a relatively innocuous choice of words. As a result you diminish the chance of creating an adversarial atmosphere.

The third sentence starter, **"What that means is…"** will lead you to your impact statement(s). Use this as an opportunity to identify what happened or could happen as a result of the behaviors(s) you're discussing.

The fourth sentence starter, **"What I need instead is…"** gives you the opportunity to pivot the conversation to identify what behaviors you'd prefer to see given a similar set of circumstances. It is, in effect, your opportunity to engage in more *specificity*. The way you handle this section of the conversation will depend on who the recipient is and what their level of tenure or experience might be.

For a newer or more inexperienced person, you may want to detail exactly what things you want them to do next time using a very detailed and specific step-by-step approach. For example, you might say something like, "First I need you to do XX. Then you need to verify YY. After you've verified YY, take the package to ZZ by 3pm."

With a more experienced or seasoned person rather than give them step-by-step directions you might be better served by giving them a specific objective or area of focus. For example what you might say to a more experienced person is: "What I need instead is to make sure that we get these orders shipped out within 24 hours of receipt of the customer's order." In this instance you're not telling them specifically *how* to do it. You're letting them know what specifically *needs to be accomplished*.

The approach that you take should be based on whom you're talking to. It's obviously important for you to know your people well enough to determine which approach would be best.

If you give a new person an objective based direction they may not know enough about the processes or procedures in your organization to know how to get there. Conversely, if you give a more seasoned person too detailed a plan to follow they might find it insulting to their level of knowledge and experience. In either case, sentence starter #4 is designed to chart a new course of action to take if the person finds himself or herself in a similar situation in the future.

Sentence starter # 5, **"What are your ideas on how..."** is where you'll bring the "20 Foot Rule" into play. Remember, the "20 Foot Rule" is designed to engage the person in charting the new course. If the person makes a great suggestion, go straight to sentence starter # 6.

The tendency for many leaders is to feel that they have to get their two cents in or have the last word. If the suggestion they make is a good one, let them run with it. When you add a suggestion behind their suggestion, you may be unintentionally signaling that you don't believe their suggestion was adequate.

If you ask them for their suggestions and they respond by saying they want to think about it, make sure to set a date and time to circle back. Their thinking about it is a good thing. It means they are taking a larger view of the situation. You may find that when you ask them for suggestions that they struggle to come up with any, or just say that they don't have any. In that case offer your own suggestion for a new set of behaviors.

The key with sentence starter # 5 is that you always want to ask them for their suggestions first, and then offer your own suggestions afterward, if necessary.

One last point on this particular sentence starter: Some situations don't lend themselves to "what are your suggestions" dialog. If for example the person needs to make sure that the alarm system is activated before they leave in the evening "what are your suggestions on how to best do that" sounds kind of dumb. In instances where there is a fundamental task that needs to be done, think K. I. S. S (Keep It Simple for Success).

Sentence starter # 6, **"Good'.   What that will do is..."** is designed to deliver a statement about the impact(s) of the recommended/suggested behaviors. This sentence starter will help to address the *"why"* question by drawing a contrast between the impacts(s) of the original behavior and the impact(s) of the suggested or recommended new behaviors.

Drawing such a contrast helps to paint a clearer "Big Picture" for the recipient of the feedback. You no doubt noticed an asterisk following the word "Good" in sentence starter # 6. There's a good reason for that. If you ask the person for suggestions on how to best meet what you need "instead" and they offer a good suggestion, saying "Good" first in your reply verbally acknowledges that you like what they've come up with. Such acknowledgement can serve as encouragement for the person and may increase the odds that they will follow their own suggestion should a similar situation rise again.

It may happen however, that you ask them for a suggestion and they don't provide one, or you end up making a suggestion, or it's a situation where soliciting a suggestion isn't appropriate. In that case skip the "Good" statement and get right to "What that will do is…" statement.

Sentence starter # 7, **"Can I count on you…?"** is where you are asking the person for their commitment to follow the new blueprint for behavior. This is a key step toward getting the person to take ownership for the new approach. Without gaining this commitment the person could leave the feedback conversation thinking; "That was your idea." or "I didn't say I was going to do it. "As a result, if a similar situation arises in the future the person, not having taken ownership of the newly prescribed behaviors, may revert back to their original behavior.

I'm guessing that right about now you're wondering "What if I ask them if I can count on them to do things differently next time and they respond by saying 'no'?" Your getting a "no" response to the commitment question could happen. If it does, avoid the urge to use an argument or threat to compel them to comply.

Instead, take a more evolved approach. If after asking them if you can count on them to do things differently next time, they reply by saying "no", simply ask them "Why not?"

Here's what I can assure you - whatever reason they give you for not agreeing to exhibit the new behavior will be found somewhere on the Non-Compliance Filter (see Chapter 3). The good news is that you now have the requisite strategies to help you deal with whatever reason they give you. The bottom line is that gaining commitment is key to getting people to change or alter their behavior and so sentence starter # 7 is a critical piece to the Feedback to Develop 1.0 process.

To summarize here are the 7 sentence starters for "Feedback to Develop 1.0"

1. "I'd like to speak to you about…" (Context)
2. "I noticed…" (Specificity)
3. "What that means is…" (Impact)
4. "What I need instead is…" (Specificity in terms of steps or objective)
5. "What suggestions do you have…" (20 Foot Rule)
6. "Good'. What that will do is…" (Impact)
7. "Can I count on you to…?" (Gaining commitment)

Feedback to Develop 1.0
Sample Scenario

Now that we have our model for Feedback to Develop 1.0. let's take it for a test drive with a sample scenario. We'll use a variation on the theme of the scenario we used earlier for Feedback to Reinforce.

The customer, Ms. Brown is upset because she's asked for a copy of her bill 3 times and she still doesn't have it. She's asked to speak to the manager (you) and you've committed to get a copy emailed to her within the hour. In addition you promised her a follow-up call to make sure she is satisfied.

The only problem is that you're headed into a meeting with your boss's boss who's visiting your office today. You explain the situation to your employee (Greg) and task him with getting a copy of Ms. Brown's bill emailed to her.

When you return from your meeting 2 hours later, you have 3 voice mails from Ms. Brown who is upset because she's still waiting for the copy of the invoice you said you'd make sure she'd receive. It seems that Greg dropped the ball on getting it emailed over to her.

This is clearly a situation where you'd be looking for a different outcome if a similar situation arises and as such would be a good candidate for Feedback to Develop 1.0. Let's plug this series of events into our Feedback to Develop 1.0 model.

1. **"Greg, I'd like to speak with you about** Ms. Brown and her needing to get a copy of her invoice ASAP. I was headed

into a meeting, and I asked you to get a copy of her bill emailed to her within the hour. "(Context)

2. **"I noticed** when I returned to my desk I had 3 voices mail messages from Ms. Brown. She's pretty upset about the fact that she still hasn't gotten a copy of her bill and now she is threatening to cancel her account. "(Specificity)

3. **"What that means is** not only have we left her with a poor impression of how well we take care of our customers, we are now also at risk of losing her business. I'm also afraid she won't have very positive things to say about us when she speaks with family and friends. "(Impact)

4. **"What I need instead**, especially where we have an escalated irate customer situation like this one, is for us to make sure that we follow through on what we commit to!" (Specificity, steps or objective)

5. **"What are your suggestions** as to how this could have been handled better? (20 Foot Rule)

    a. Greg: "I'm sorry. I got caught up on a conference call and just forgot all about it. Next time I'll make sure I just get right to it. "

6. **"Good. What that will do is** make sure that our customers can believe that when we say we'll do something, we'll do it. I also think your suggestion of getting right to it will help make sure that things don't accidentally end up falling through the cracks." (Impact)

7. **"Can I count on you** to do that the next time a situation like this comes up?" (Gain commitment)

    a. Greg: "Sure. "

Now let's play the same scenario out with a twist. Imagine the conversation being the same all the way up to the point where you ask for Greg's commitment and instead of saying "Sure", Greg says "No. "

You: "Can I count on you to do that the next time a situation like this comes up?" (Gain commitment)

Greg: "No. "

You: "Why Not?"

Greg: "Well, the conference call that I was on is one that you told me was mandatory for me to be part of. I didn't want to get in trouble for missing it. "

You: "That conference call is important, but irate escalated customers should always take priority. So if a similar situation comes up again, I want you to focus on resolving the escalated customer situation first. Can I count on you to do that?" (Gain commitment)

Greg: "Ok. "

Feedback to Develop 1.0
Practicum

Now it's your turn!

I'd like you to think of 3 instances in the past week where someone in your professional or personal life has done something that would warrant you providing them with Feedback to Develop 1.0. Again as before with Feedback to Reinforce, try to include at least one personal example.

What we'll do for each scenario (just as we did before with Feedback to Reinforce) is break down the context, specifics and impact(s) of the behaviors in question. Then we'll actually have you translate that information into the model for Feedback to Develop 1.0. Finally, as we did before, we'll get you to speak the feedback out loud and make a note of how long it took.

Real World Scenario #1 for Feedback to Develop 1.0

Write down a brief answer to each of these questions

What was it about?

When did it take place?

What specific behaviors do you want altered/changed?

What was /were the impact(s) of the behavior(s)?

What are your suggestions for different behaviors?

What would be the impact of the newly prescribed behaviors?

Now plug Real World Scenario #1 into the Feedback to Develop 1.0 model.

Scenario #1

1) "_____(person's name), I'd like to speak with you a moment about...

2) "I noticed..."

3) "What that means is..."

4) "What I need instead is..."

5) "What are your suggestions for…"

6) "Good'. What that will do is…

7) "Can I count on you to…"

Now read the scenario out loud. How long did it take?

Real World Scenario #2 for Feedback to Develop 1.0

Write down a brief answer to each of these questions

What was it about?

When did it take place?

What specific behaviors do you want altered/changed?

What was /were the impact(s) of the behavior(s)?

What are your suggestions for different behaviors?

What would be the impact of the newly prescribed behaviors?

Now plug Scenario #2 into the Feedback to Develop 1.0 model.

Scenario # 2

1) "_____(person's name), I'd like to speak with you a moment about…

2) "I noticed…"

3) "What that means is…"

4) "What I need instead is…"

5) "What are your suggestions for…"

6) "Good'. What that will do is…

7) "Can I count on you to…"

Now read the scenario out loud. How long did it take?

Real World Scenario #3 for Feedback to Develop 1.0

Write down a brief answer to each of these questions

What was it about?

When did it take place?

What specific behaviors do you want altered/changed?

What was /were the impact(s) of the behavior(s)?

What are your suggestions for different behaviors?

What would be the impact of the newly prescribed behaviors?

Now plug Scenario #3 into the Feedback to Develop 1.0 model.

Scenario #3

1) "_____(person's name), I'd like to speak with you a moment about...

2) "I noticed..."

3) "What that means is..."

4) "What I need instead is..."

5) "What are your suggestions for…"

6) "Good'. What that will do is…

7) "Can I count on you to…"

Now read the scenario out loud. How long did it take?

Notes on Feedback to Develop 1.0

Using your own verbiage?

Great! Remember the point is to make sure all the critical components (context, specificity, impact, and commitment) are present. *Still bouncing around a bit from impact to specificity and vs. versa?*

Again, that is to be expected as sometimes the course of the conversation may call for it. With Feedback to Develop 1.0 however, there is something important to remember.

Think of Feedback to Develop 1.0 having 2 sections. **Section 1** being the description and impact(s) of the observed behavior (sentence starters # 1 - # 3). **Section 2** dealing with the newly prescribed behaviors, their impact(s), and gaining commitment (sentence starters # 4 - # 7).

Always finish Section 1 (even if you bounce between sentence starters #1 -3), *before* moving to Section 2. Having a clear delineation between observed behaviors and newly prescribed behaviors increases the effectiveness of your feedback. Not doing so can make for a confusing conversation, leaving the person less certain about what the point of the feedback is.

You'll notice that there aren't any "disclaimer" statements at the beginning of the feedback.

Examples of disclaimer statements would be: "Don't take this the wrong way" or "This isn't a big deal", or "Just hear me out. "These types of statements give the impression that you're anticipating a confrontation, which, by the way is the best way to guarantee yourself one. Statements like these could also unintentionally send the message that the feedback recipient shouldn't take what you're saying seriously. In short, you don't have to apologize in advance for giving feedback that is professional, helpful, and designed to make the person a stronger contributor to the aims and goals of your organization.

Avoid asking the person "why" unless it comes after a response to your commitment question.
There can be a temptation, especially right after you describe the observed behavior to ask "why did you do that?" or "why didn't you do that?"Asking the why question this early in your feedback interaction can set an accusatory tone.

As a result, the recipient of your feedback is likely to adopt a defensive posture limiting their ability to process what you're saying and the likelihood that the behavior will change.

When you ask the commitment question the response you're looking for should be a clear verbal affirmative.
When you ask the "Can I count on you to..." question, getting responses like "yes", "sure", "ok", "no problem", etc. , is the goal.

If you get no verbal response to your commitment question or responses that are vague such as "If you say so", "Whatever", "I don't have a choice do I?" acknowledge the non-committal answer by saying something like, "I'm not getting the sense that this is something you're really committing to. Is there something I'm missing?". Then listen for the underlying issue(s) that will, again, probably be somewhere on your Non-Compliance Filter. Then propose the appropriate strategy and ask for his or her commitment again.

Repeat this process until you uncover the real issue and gain a commitment or until you come to the conclusion that it may be time to start reducing the number of passengers on the bus.

Leaving Feedback to Develop 1.0 open ended with no definitive affirmative commitment will almost assuredly mean that you'll have to have this conversation again.

Remember, the point of Feedback to Develop 1.0 is to do just that – Develop.
As such, it is an essential tool in helping your organization gain and sustain operational excellence.

Delivering Effective Feedback in 2 Minutes or Less
Feedback to Develop 2.0

Feedback to Develop 2.0 is designed to give feedback when some part of the person's behaviors meet your expectations and should be reinforced, but there is also room for development in other aspects of the behavior.

A person making incremental progress toward a goal, for example, would be a good candidate for the Feedback to Develop 2.0 model. A person who completed part of a task but not all of it would also be someone who would be able to benefit from Feedback to Develop 2.0.

The architecture for Feedback to Develop 2.0 is very similar to Feedback to Develop 1.0 with a couple of notable twists. Feedback to Develop 2.0 also has seven sentence starters.

1. "I'd like to speak to you about…"
2. "I like/appreciate…"
3. "That's important because…"
4. "Going forward,…"
5. "What are your suggestions…"
6. "Good˙ What that will do is…"
7. "Can I count on you to…?"

You'll notice in the Feedback to Develop 2.0 model, you find a blend of Feedback to Reinforce (steps 1-3) and Feedback to Develop 1.0 (steps 4-7)

You'll also note that sentence starter # 4 is different in 2.0 than in 1.0. In Feedback to Develop 1.0, sentence starter # 4 reads "What I need instead…" which implies a more wholesale change in behavior. In Feedback to Develop 2.0 sentence starter # 4 reads, "Going forward, ..." which implies we'll keep some of what we have and add or tweak other behaviors.

Using Feedback to Develop 2.0 is important because it acknowledges incremental improvement and/or behaviors that are on the right path. It serves to encourage the individual to continue their positive progress. Withholding praise until someone "crosses the finish line" could lead to that person slowing his or her forward progress or giving up altogether.

I'll spare you the details associated with each individual sentence starter. We've covered them thoroughly in our discussions on Feedback to Reinforce and Feedback to Develop 1.0.

Since Feedback to Develop 2.0 model is a hybrid of Feedback to Reinforce and Feedback to Develop 1.0, let's just summarize those sentence starters here, identifying which critical components of feedback they will help you address. Feedback to Develop 2.0 model

1. "I'd like to speak to you about..." (Context)
2. "I like/appreciate..." (Specificity)
3. "That's important because..." (Impact)
4. "Going forward,..." (Specificity of process or objective)
5. "What suggestions do you have..." (20 Foot Rule)
6. "Good'. What that will do is..." (Impact)
7. "Can I count on you to...?" (Gaining Commitment)

Now let's plug a scenario into Feedback to Develop 2.0

Your employee Greg consistently generates very thorough and accurate monthly productivity reports but last month's report was submitted 2 days after the submission deadline.

1. **"Greg, I'd like to speak with you about** last months productivity report"(Context)
2. **"I appreciate** that it reflected your usual degree of thoroughness and accuracy"(Specificity)
3. **"That's important because** thorough and accurate reports help us stay on track with our performance and let's us know when we might need to make course corrections to keep our productivity levels high"(Impact)
4. **"Going forward**, I really need you to get those reports in by the deadline. This last report came in a couple of days late" (Specificity, steps or objective)
5. **"What are your suggestions** on what you can do to make sure that we always get those reports in on time (20 Foot Rule)
   a. Greg: "I'm sorry about that. I was waiting on some information from Shift 1, but I didn't know the supervisor that I usually get it from was on vacation at the end of the month.
   I'll talk to the supervisors on all the shifts and ask them to have a person as a back-up that can get me their shift reports just in case they aren't there for some reason."
6. **"Good. What that will do is** give us the best possible shot to keep our reputation of meeting deadlines in tact. It will also probably be helpful for the shift supervisors to have a back-up plan so they won't be unnecessarily stressed out in case they are out of the office around deadline time." (Impact)
7. **"Can I count on you** to follow up with the shift supervisors on your plan?" (Gain commitment)
   a. **Greg**: "Yes you can. "

Feedback to Develop 2.0
Practicum

Now it's your turn!

I'd like you to think of 3 instances in the past week where someone in your professional or personal life has done something that would warrant you providing them with Feedback to Develop 2.0. Again as before with Feedback to Reinforce, try to include at least one personal example.

What we'll do for each scenario (just as we've done twice before with Feedback to Reinforce and Feedback to Develop 1.0) is break down the context, specifics and impact(s) of the behaviors in question. Then we'll actually have you translate that information into the model for Feedback to Develop 2.0. Finally, as we did before, we'll get you to speak the feedback out loud and make a note of how long it took.

Real World Scenario #1 for Feedback to Develop 2.0

Write down a brief answer to each of these questions

What was it about?

When did it take place?

What specific behaviors do you want altered/changed?

What was /were the impact(s) of the behavior(s)?

What are your suggestions for different behaviors?

What would be the impact of the newly prescribed behaviors?

Now plug Real World Scenario #1 into the Feedback to Develop 2.0 model.

Scenario # 1

1) "_____(person's name), I'd like to speak with you a moment about...

2) "I like/appreciate..."

3) "That's important because..."

4) "Going forward..."

5) "What are your suggestions for..."

6) "Good'. What that will do is..."

7) "Can I count on you to..."

Now read the scenario out loud. How long did it take?

Real World Scenario #2 for Feedback to Develop 2.0

Write down a brief answer to each of these questions

What was it about?

When did it take place?

What specific behaviors do you want altered/changed?

What was /were the impact(s) of the behavior(s)?

What are your suggestions for different behaviors?

What would be the impact of the newly prescribed behaviors?

Now plug Real World Scenario #2 into the Feedback to Develop 2.0 model.

Scenario # 2

1) "_____(person's name), I'd like to speak with you a moment about...

2) "I like/appreciate..."

3) "That's important because..."

4) "Going forward..."

5) "What are your suggestions for…"

6) "Good'. What that will do is…

7) "Can I count on you to…"

Now read the scenario out loud. How long did it take?

Real World Scenario #3 for Feedback to Develop 2.0

Write down a brief answer to each of these questions

What was it about?

When did it take place?

What specific behaviors do you want altered/changed?

What was /were the impact(s) of the behavior(s)?

What are your suggestions for different behaviors?

What would be the impact of the newly prescribed behaviors?

Now plug Real World Scenario #3 into the Feedback to Develop 2.0 model.

Scenario # 3

1) "_____(person's name), I'd like to speak with you a moment about...

2) "I like/appreciate..."

3) "That's important because..."

4) "Going forward..."

5) "What are your suggestions for…"

6) "Good'. What that will do is…

7) "Can I count on you to…"

Now read the scenario out loud. How long did it take?

Notes on Feedback to Develop 2.0

You'll notice that we're not using the words "however", or "but" in step 4.
Rather, we use the phrase "Going forward...". The reason we avoid using the words "however" and "but" is because they are *eraser* words. That means when they are used they functionally *erase* everything that was said before them.

For example if I say, "you did a good job, however..." it's clear that what I really came to talk about is not the "good job" you did. What I really came to talk to you about is what comes after "however. "The word "but" has the same effect. It's like when someone says, "I have some good news and some bad news. "All of us intuitively know that the real message being delivered is the "bad" news.

Remember, this is a great tool for acknowledging progress
We've said it before and we'll say it again. You don't have to wait for someone to get all the way to the finish line before you encourage them and coach them with feedback.

Praising incremental progress often fuels the energy for continued progress.

Feedback FAQs
Where should you give Feedback?

Feedback, when being delivered to an individual is in essence a performance based conversation, and as such should be conducted with an eye toward privacy and confidentiality.

This doesn't mean that you have to sequester you and the recipient of the feedback every time you have a conversation about their performance. It does mean however, that there should be some measure of privacy afforded to the conversation. Preferably, your feedback should only be audible to you and the person to whom you're providing the feedback.

Delivering feedback to a particular individual should not take place in meetings with others, on the workroom floor, in front of customers, etc. Even if the feedback is Feedback to Reinforce, it's important to remember that not everyone likes to be the recipient of public praise.

Delivering Feedback to Develop should be delivered with the same considerations in mind. Delivering Feedback to Develop in a setting where others can hear any part of the conversation amounts to a public flogging, no matter how minor or insignificant you feel the conversation is. The fact that you're having the conversation makes it significant by default. Having it where others can witness or hear it is wholly inappropriate.

Sometimes leaders make the mistake of providing Feedback to Develop to an individual by embedding it in a conversation with the entire team. This often happens because:

1. The leader, for one reason or another, is uncomfortable with having a one on one conversation with the person for whom the feedback is intended, or
2. The leader feels like the intended recipient of feedback in the group will "get it" and know who's really being addressed and that throwing out feedback "hints" out in the meeting will save the leader from having to take the time out later to have a one on one conversation with the person.

What usually ends up happening however is that the entire group ends up being confused. No one really knows to whom the feedback actually is being directed. As a result, team members find themselves in the meeting thinking, "Is he or she talking about *me*?" Ironically, it's not unusual for the intended recipient of the feedback to miss the whole point.

There is a place and time to deliver feedback to the team as a team, but using team settings to covertly deliver feedback to an individual usually ends up being totally ineffective. It can also demonstrate what is perceived to be a lack of courage on the part of the leader.

The moral to the story here is that feedback for specific individuals should be delivered in settings that foster some modicum of privacy.

Feedback FAQs

What's the best method for giving feedback to persons who are remotely located?

While giving feedback face to face is the ideal setting, it's not always possible. In today's environment, many leaders have team members that are located across the country or even across the globe. I am often asked about situations like these and whether it's OK to give the feedback via e-mail. The answer is yes, but only as a *last* resort!

When you aren't in the same physical location as the person to whom you wish to provide feedback (whether it's Feedback to Reinforce or Feedback to Develop) here's how I'd rank the options.

Option # 1: Video Conference

Video conferencing would be my primary suggestion for remote feedback conversations. It allows for the very important communicative elements of tone of voice and body language to be in play. There is something about the ability to make eye contact that adds a level of seriousness and importance to the conversation.

There are numerous video conferencing tools available. Many of these services are available at no charge.

Option # 2: Telephone

If the video conferencing option is not available or practical, the next best thing is to make an old fashioned phone call. Even though you won't have the benefit of visual contact, your tone of voice can help you deliver not just the text of your feedback message, but the sentiment of the message as well.

The phone call also allows for an immediate exchange of information, which may be helpful especially if you're delivering Feedback to Develop.

Option # 3: E-mail
If and only if option 1 and 2 are unavailable to you (which is pretty unlikely, by the way) utilizing e-mail as a forum of discussion for feedback could be considered an option.

I'm listing e-mail as the third option because without the benefit of visual and aural cues and the immediacy of exchange present in the first two options, feedback delivered via e-mail could be open to a great deal more interpretation (or misinterpretation). The recipient could be "reading in" intent or meaning that is not part of your message. Also, because there is no forum for immediate exchange, any misinterpretations that take place can have time to take root. This can be problematic especially in the case of Feedback to Develop as a misinterpreted message could result in more stressed or confrontational communication going forward.

That being said, e-mail does have one benefit that the other two options don't inherently have – instant documentation of the interaction that can be easily referenced. My suggestion is to use e-mail as a supporting tool in your feedback rather than the method of choice.

Use e-mail to send a summary of your feedback to the recipient. This will allow them and you to readily access and refer back to the feedback message. This is a good idea even as a follow-up to face-to-face feedback conversations. The more information someone has about his or her level of performance in situations large or small, the better able they will be to stay on track and help you sustain high levels of operational excellence.

You'll notice that in this discourse about preferred options for delivering feedback remotely, that I don't distinguish between Feedback to Reinforce and Feedback to Develop. I encourage you to be consistent irrespective of the nature of the feedback.

If you have a remote employee/team member and you tend to call to give Feedback to Reinforce but tend to generate an e-mail to deliver Feedback to Develop, you'll be creating an unhelpful dynamic. The person while looking forward to your call may begin to receive your e-mails with a sense of dread, even when there is no reason for them to. So whatever options you choose to employ to deliver feedback from afar, be consistent.

Feedback FAQs
How often should you deliver feedback?

If I'd begun this discourse on feedback by stating that you should be giving feedback at least 60 times a week, you probably would have closed the book and started wondering what else you could have spent your money on. But now that you know that you can deliver most of your feedback in 2 minutes (most in significantly less than 2 minutes) it might seem more realistic.

Let's do the math!

60 Feedback sessions X 2 minutes (or less) = 120 minutes/2 hours (or less) per week.

That means in a 40 hour week (which would be a welcome departure for most leaders) feedback would make up 5% or less of your time each week. That's not a substantial investment in terms of quantity of time, but it's guaranteed to yield great returns.

To be merciful, how about your committing to 40 feedback conversations per week (which would make up 3% or less of your time)? You can work your way up from there.

I can also assure you that when you shift your paradigm to delivering feedback with a more proactive mindset, there will be another welcome benefit. You'll find that there will soon begin to be less "fires to fight" and fewer crises to manage.

Every moment a leader dedicates to giving quality feedback is critical to the ongoing success of the organization. However, It requires a commitment on behalf of the leader. Feedback must become and stay a Big Rock.

What commitment to delivering quality feedback are *you* willing to make?

Feedback FAQs
How will they react?

If you begin to start offering this increased volume of feedback, it's likely that your team members will wonder what's going on. They may start thinking that you must have attended a training seminar or read a new book lately.

There may even be some skepticism initially. The skepticism will exist because they've "seen this movie" before. Unfortunately, the movie always ends the same way; the leader's behavior over time reverts back to the same old ways. The key here, then, is for you to be consistent over the long term.

Once your team buys into the fact that this shift in paradigm toward the consistent and frequent delivery of feedback is not a temporary shift, their skepticism will begin to fade and will soon be replaced with something else; expectations that the new paradigm will continue rather than fade.

There is some irony here. It seems that one of the best ways for you to help your organization sustain operational excellence is for you to sustain your own behaviors associated with effective coaching and feedback.

Consistently effective leadership then is the best track to consistent and sustained operational excellence.

Feedback FAQs
Should I be documenting my Feedback?

Consider making it a point to document your feedback conversations with your team members. Unfortunately the term "documentation" is too often used in reference to taking steps necessary to get someone "off the bus." Documenting feedback discussions may obviously serve that purpose in some cases.

However, the bigger picture as it relates to documenting feedback is that it provides you with the reference point as to the level of proficiency at which your team member is operating at any given point in time. Such documentation not only charts problematic issues, but progress and positive performance as well.

Additionally, when the recipient of your feedback understands that there will be a written record of the conversation, it adds weight to the conversation. What is said may or may not be remembered, but what is written remains.

Consider creating a Feedback Report form that includes the following:

- Employee/Team Member Name
- Date/Time of Observed Behavior
- Where Observed Behavior Took Place
- Specific Behavior Observed
- Impact(s) of Observed Behavior
- Employee/Team Members Suggestions (if any)
- Your Suggestions (if any)
- Performance Observed By
- Feedback Delivered By

- Feedback Delivered (date/time)
- Date/Time Scheduled for Follow-up (if applicable)

You can see an example of how such a form might be used and download a PDF of a Feedback Report Form I created for your use by going to this specific page on my website: greggray. com/ *gtst*.

Feedback
More "Model" Applications

In addition to the feedback interactions we've discussed so far, there are other applications for the feedback models we've shared. Here are just a few.

Monthly performance talks and annual performance reviews.
Utilize the models here to give a big picture roll-up of the person's activities, the impact of their performance on the organization and where necessary to chart a course for their professional development. This could include everything from suggesting better deadline management, executing better follow-up, and even taking classes to sharpen or gain important job skills.

Employee Recognition Write-ups
Sometimes, the employee that receives the highest level of recognition isn't necessarily the employee that's achieved the most, or had the most impact on the organization. Rather it is usually the employee whose write-up submission had an author that did the best job of detailing the employee's accomplishments (specificity) and chronicling what those accomplishments meant to the organization (impact).

Consider using the approach from Feedback to Reinforce as a framework to build upon when submitting an employee for special recognition, or use it to make the case to someone that you should be receiving such recognition.

Letters of Recommendation

Here's another place where focusing on specificity and impact can prove helpful. Hiring managers, college admissions professionals, and others responsible for choosing candidates for a particular role or job appreciate being supplied with specifics. The specifics play an important role when considering whether to bring someone on board or even whether they should be promoted. Past performance is a good indicator of future performance.

Assessing a job candidate's interviewing performance

When debriefing someone who got a job they applied for, you can actually strengthen them as a new employee by telling them specifically why you chose them. This kind of information reinforces what it is you'll be looking for from them as they begin their new role.

When debriefing someone who doesn't get the job or position, focusing specifically on how they may have fallen short in the interview and how that impacted your decision can serve to make the person a stronger candidate in the future.

Disciplinary Documents

If you find that is has become necessary to implement disciplinary procedures, documenting the specifics and resulting impacts of the unacceptable behavior can paint a clearer picture as to why the discipline was called for. It also provides you as a leader with a defensible position going forward in case the discipline needs to progress further; up to and including reducing the number of passengers on the bus.

Feedback: More Important Stuff
"Getting" Expectations and Feedback from Others

Sustaining operational excellence is not just a factor of you communicating clear expectations and delivering effective feedback for your team. It is also a matter of you being clear as to what is expected of *you* and your receiving feedback to ensure that you're on the right track.

If you find in your position that you are either unclear on what's expected of you or you're concerned that you're not getting enough feedback from the person(s) to whom you report, there's a remedy for that.

Consider altering the script from the Feedback to Develop models to communicate that you need more clarity on what's expected of you:

1. "I'd like to speak with you about my performance. "(Context)
2. "I noticed that we haven't had a chance to get together and discuss your expectations of me." (Specificity)
3. "I want to make sure that I'm focused on the things you believe to be most important" (Impact)
4. "I'd like to sit down sometime soon (suggest a specific date/timeframe) to make sure I'm clear on what you expect from me" (Specificity of objective)
5. "When do you think that might be possible?" (Gain Commitment)

Similarly you can use a variation of the Feedback to Develop model to *get* feedback:

1. "I'd like to speak with you about my performance. "(Context)
2. "I noticed that we haven't gotten together in a while to discuss how I'm doing." (Specificity)
3. "I feel like I'm on the right track, but I want to be sure and getting your feedback would be very helpful." (Impact)
4. "I'd like to start sitting down with you periodically (suggest a specific schedule) to get your feedback and make sure I'm on the right track." (Specificity of objective)
5. "Do you think that might be possible?" (Gaining Commitment)

Feedback: More Important Stuff
Feedback as a Teaching Tool

In addition to the obvious benefits of delivering effective and efficient feedback that we've outlined so far, there is another subtle but powerful outcome. When you focus on context, specificity, and impact in your interactions with your team, you encourage them, by your example, to do the same.

You'll find over time, for example, that persons who have suggestions for doing something differently will be more likely to include specific details in their suggestions. They will also begin to include what impact(s) they believe their suggested ideas will have on the organization. When they don't provide specifics and impact statements, you should send them back to the drawing board.

You will also, by your example, be teaching ascending leaders in your organization how effective leaders communicate with members of their teams. When you create an atmosphere where this kind of detailed communication is the norm you will at the same time be creating an atmosphere where sustained operational excellence becomes a very achievable objective.

Feedback: More Important Stuff
A Few Very Important Things to Remember

As you focus or refocus your efforts on giving feedback, there are a few important things to keep in mind:

- Everyone is entitled to feedback... even the people you don't like.
- The most effective feedback is always preceded by clearly communicated expectations.
- Know that people are comparing the feedback you give... consistency is key.
- Make your feedback as timely as possible.
- Praise progress.
- Don't hesitate to ask for a commitment to change.
- Focus on behaviors, not attitudes.
- No one likes "public floggings".
- Some people are uncomfortable with "public praise".
- "However" and "But" are eraser words... avoid using them.
- Don't give up on giving feedback.
- Practice won't make you perfect, but it will make you better.
- These strategies can work outside of the work place.

CHAPTER 9

BEWARE THE "THE DEAL BREAKER"

As you read through the chapter on Feedback, there's a chance that at least once you had one of the following thoughts:

- *"That sentence starter seems like it would put the person on the defensive. . "*
- *"This is easier said than done..."*
- *"Nice idea, but too simplistic for some of the difficult people I have to deal with..."*

I feel pretty certain that you probably had one of these thoughts because every time I've ever conducted seminars on feedback, I've heard these and similar comments from participants; usually throughout the seminar. What I share with them is what I'll share with you now.

There is a "Deal Breaker" that has the potential to derail any of your efforts toward delivering feedback. The same Deal Breaker can also significantly impact morale in your organization. This Deal Breaker, in fact, has the ability to compromise any strategy you put in place to sustain operational excellence.

So "What is this all powerful Deal Breaker", you ask?

To explain it to you, I first need you to answer a couple of questions.

Question #1
Of all the activity in your organization that has taken place over the past 30 days, what % of the time were the people in your organization doing the right things (i. e. activities that would justify you delivering Feedback to Reinforce)?

Write that % here:_____

Now before we go to the next question, a comment or 2 about the % you just wrote down.

If you wrote down an answer that is less than 70%, chances are:

1. Your organization is on the verge of collapse. It is virtually impossible for any organization to have 30% or more of all it's activity be the wrong activities and be able to sustain itself for any significant period of time, or
2. More likely, you just aren't paying attention and/or your time and attention is being monopolized by crises and problems.

Now on to Question #2:
What % of all the feedback you've delivered in the last 30 days has been Feedback to Reinforce (the feedback formally known as positive feedback)?

Write that % here:_____

Here's the deal…

If the answers from both questions don't match, it's highly unlikely that your efforts toward feedback will be effective with any level of consistency.

If for example, the first answer is 80-90% (which is what the overwhelming majority of seminar attendees answer) and the answer to Question #2 is any % less (many seminar attendees identify the answer to Question #2 as 35-50%), there will be a significant disconnect that will be difficult to reconcile in the minds of your team members. Put another way, if 90% of the time what your team members are doing are the right things, but only 40% of your feedback is Feedback to Reinforce, it will create an interesting and difficult dynamic. Your team members will come to expect that when you approach them to discuss their performance, there's a better than even chance that you're there to tell them about something that they have done wrong. It's not difficult to understand why in scenarios like this that team members' default posture regarding performance discussions would be a defensive one.

The team members begin to form the opinion rather quickly that what gets your attention is not what they do right, but what they do wrong. As a result, over time the percentage answer to Question #1 will likely begin to go into a steady decline.

So what's the point here? How do you disarm the Deal Breaker?

The point is to create an environment in which the answer to question number 2 matches the answer to Question #1. If 9 out of 10 activities in your organization are the right activities, then 90% of your feedback should be Feedback to Reinforce. If you can create such an atmosphere, you can positively shift the paradigm around feedback in your organization.

Team members will begin to anticipate an acknowledgment of good work when you approach them. As this becomes the case, the need for a more defensive posture will begin to diminish.

There is also the likelihood that when you do need to deliver Feedback to Develop, it will be better received especially if you take care to incorporate all the components we outlined (clear expectations, context, specificity, and impact).

Further, if you can consistently get the answer to Question #2 to equal the answer to Question #1, you can diminish the urge to use the "Sandwich Approach" to giving feedback.

The Sandwich Approach to giving feedback suggests that if you have to provide "negative" feedback, you should begin by saying something complimentary before you deliver the message you really came to deliver. You're then supposed to say something complimentary at the end so the conversation will end on a positive note.

Here is a highly scientific graphic illustrating the 3 step Sandwich Approach:

THE SANDWICH APPROACH

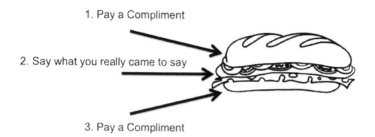

1. Pay a Compliment

2. Say what you really came to say

3. Pay a Compliment

The problem with the Sandwich Approach is that recipients of feedback will become uncertain as to what you're really there to talk about. Even worse, after the "complimentary set up" they'll likely be thinking, "Okay, what did you really come here to tell me?"

It's similar to the way we respond when we hear someone say, "I have some good news and some bad news". We all intuitively understand that what the person really came to give us is the bad news.

Every feedback conversation you have with someone should stand on its own merit. To "sandwich" feedback or use the good news/bad news approach is, in my opinion, manipulative. Said in another less delicate way, the sandwich approach is full of baloney.

If 90% of the activities in an organization are meeting expectations and 90% of your conversations about performance fall into the category of Feedback to Reinforce, the leader won't need to set people up for Feedback to Develop. The team will understand that the leader is paying attention to the whole of their performance. They will also believe that the leader is more invested in catching them doing things right than in catching them doing things wrong.

If you want your organization to be able to sustain operational excellence, then minimize the impact of the Deal Breaker by working consistently to make sure the answer to Question #2 equals the answer to Question #1.

CHAPTER 10

COMMUNICATION CONSIDERATIONS

To write a book on leadership and not include a chapter on communication seems almost counterintuitive. The fact is though that this entire book has communication as its cornerstone. From clear expectations, to the 20 Foot Rule, to feedback, it's all about keeping an effective pipeline of communication open between the leadership of the organization and the members of the organization.

While we won't be reviewing everything we've already covered in the book again in this chapter, there are some considerations around communications that I think we should explore a bit. Principally at the request (actually desperate plea) of numerous people who knew I'd be authoring a book on leadership.

Communication Consideration #1

Err on the side of sharing too much rather than too little information with your team

All organizations are better capable of sustaining operational excellence when the members of the team feel kept in the loop as to what's going on in the organization. While knowledge is power, *shared* knowledge is *empowering*.

The interesting thing about people, including the people on your team, is that if they don't have all the information, they'll soon begin to speculate about the information they know they are missing. If that speculation is allowed to linger, whether it is correct or not, it will soon begin to be perceived as reality. Any later efforts to dispel incorrect information will be difficult at best and met with suspicion at worst.

If you have information that is not shareable and people inquire about it, it's better to answer that you are not permitted to share it and why than to say "I don't know". Integrity matters.

As a leader in your organization, make it a Big Rock to keep your team as well informed as possible. That means good news and bad news alike. Team members respect leaders who are willing to "put all their cards on the table". Such leaders are perceived not only to be trustworthy and courageous, but people who others are willing to follow.

Communication Consideration #2
Minimize "Crisis-Based" communication

Try to create an environment where the wide majority of your communication does not take place during times of crisis. The effectiveness of communication that takes place in times of crisis tends to suffer because:

1. It is rarely long term focused in scope. More often, crisis based communication is about putting out *this* particular fire. As a result, it tends to fall short on the *preventive* paradigm scale.
2. People are often more likely to take a defensive posture during crisis based communication. Deflecting blame becomes as big (or bigger) a part of the discourse as is dealing with the issue at hand.

In a nutshell, crisis based communication is, generally speaking, more focused on ending the crisis at hand than on avoiding similar crises in the future. It is also typically so exhausting that afterwards people tend to retreat back to their corners to recuperate.

In the case of large scale organizational changes especially in the case of downsizing, pull the team together as soon as possible to explain the "What's, Who's, Where's, Why's, When's, and How's" and answer questions as thoroughly as possible. Large-scale change typically translates into large-scale anxiety amongst members of the organization. Being as open, honest, and accessible as soon as possible is your best option. To do otherwise will have the effect of impeding the organization's focus on the work at hand.

There is obviously no way to eliminate crisis-based communication. It comes long with the territory of being a part of any organization.

The key here is to tilt the scale towards proactive communication. Focus on getting out in front of issues and potential crises and on developing preventive strategies, not just fixes.

Communication Consideration #3

Avoid doing a few things done with email that don't go over well with the team

1. All of your emails aren't URGENT. When all of your emails are marked as urgent, the reality is that your team eventually stops mentally processing any of them as urgent. After a while they may even be regarded as low priority. Instead, use the "subject line" to communicate the urgency of time sensitive issues.

2. CC only the people who *need* to know the stuff in your message. When you regularly cc the whole world on your email messages, it comes across as either over the top self-promotion, covering your backside, or using the distribution list because you're too lazy to send the message only to the select few people for whom the message is relevant or important.

3. More on CC. Don't cc the world on the back and forth between you and another individual. Only involve the rest of us if you actually need us to do something. Otherwise, take it off line, or on-line only between the interested parties.

4. Use "Reply-All" sparingly. Just because a message was sent to you as part of a group doesn't mean we all want or need to see your response to the sender. Unless the sender directs you to "reply-all", "reply" only is more often than not plenty good enough.

As we discussed in the chapter on feedback, email is not your best option for delivering feedback – especially if it is feedback to develop. Pick up the phone or, better yet, just walk over and have the conversation.

Communication Consideration #4
Run effective meetings

Most people in most organizations describe meetings as being the bane of their existence. Very few people regularly describe meetings with any measurable degree of positivity. It's not that meetings are unimportant (well maybe some of them). It's more that they aren't often run very well.

Here are a few quick tips (or considerations) to help bolster the effectiveness of your meetings and how they are received.

Start and end your meetings on time
No matter how many people are (or are not) present at the appointed start time, get the meeting rolling. The people who were on time will appreciate it and the people who were late (especially those folks who are habitually late) will get the point.

Always create a meeting agenda and send it to attendees in advance of the meeting
This helps team member better prepare for the meeting. It may also help them determine whether the meeting is important enough for them to attend.

Put the Big Rocks at the "top" of the agenda
If you make a point of putting the Big Rock (most important) agenda items at the top of the agenda there are a couple of benefits.

1. It provides even more incentive for meeting attendees to be on time.

2. If time runs short in your meeting, your prioritization of the Big Rock items helps ensure that you will have covered the most important stuff.

Often meetings begin with statements like "let's cover a few small items before we get to the big stuff on the agenda" (an agenda, by the way that sometimes hadn't been sent in advance to the team). Somehow the "small" items always become bigger items and as a result, the meeting time is extended, or worse, another meeting has to be scheduled to cover the actual big items.

Moral to the meeting agenda story: Put the Big Rocks in the jar (on the agenda) first.

Give team members a heads up on info they need to bring to the meeting

If someone is responsible for an item(s) on the agenda (updates, reports, etc.) let them know ample time in advance for them to prepare. Springing a request for an update on someone during the meeting is not only less than effective (in that the quality of the update may be compromised with this last minute notice), it's also discourteous and in bad form.

Record Meeting Minutes

When minutes are recorded, it gives you a record of any action items and to whom those items were assigned. This creates a greater sense of accountability for the persons in question.

Having recorded minutes from the meeting also allows key persons who could not attend have the benefit of the same information as those who were present.

Avoid using general meetings as forums to solve problems or as strategy sessions

Instead form sub-committees or task forces to come up with recommendations or proposals. Then schedule a spot on the agenda of the next appropriate meeting for the presentation of those recommendations and or proposals.

Trying to do too much problem solving or strategizing in the general meeting setting often tends to bog the meeting down – especially if attendees weren't aware that this type of effort was going to be part of the meeting. (Hint: send out agendas in advance)

Familiarize yourself with "Robert's Rules of Order"

Consider having the leaders in your organization (including you) become versed or at least acquainted with "Robert's Rules of Order". It is a time-tested methodology for conducting effective meetings and is a great source for the development of leaders.

Communication Consideration #5
If you're not sure...

If you're ever uncertain as to how effective communications are in your organization, use the 20 Foot Rule.

CHAPTER 11

WHY MOTIVATING OTHERS IS OVERRATED

At the conclusion of seminars and keynote addresses, I'm often asked what suggestions I have for motivating a group of employees, a sports team, a group of volunteers, etc.

This is a fair inquiry to be sure.

Leaders from every corner have posed this question because at some point in time they find themselves faced with a team/group that they feel is lacking in motivation and perhaps even struggling with low morale. Their concern is that this lack of motivation could negatively impact the organization's ability to consistently perform at a high level. Low morale could also have a detrimental effect on employee/manager relationships and employee turnover rates.

Given all this, you may be asking yourself why in the world I would suggest that spending time and energy on trying to motivate these folks might **not** be the best use of your time.

Here's my take on the whole motivation thing – it's a little overrated, and here's why…

After having had the opportunity to speak with literally tens of thousands of people representing dozens of industries public and private, including employees, volunteers, athletes, and students, I've become totally convinced of one very clear fact – These people were all motivated when they showed up the very first time. In other words, they all brought their own motivation with them.

Well if you accept that little premise as being accurate (that these folks started out motivated), then perhaps rather than spending time, money, energy, and resources on trying to *re*-motivate them, maybe we would be better served by spending some time determining what in our environment served to *de-motivate* them along the way. Trying to motivate people in a de-motivating environment is a lost cause and a colossal waste of time and resources.

My belief is that if you spend time identifying and then acting to remove the de-motivating elements that exist in your organizational environment, the motivation that people showed up with in the first place will likely begin to re-emerge on it's own.

So here's the *real* question: "How do we find out what's de-motivating people around here?" The solution I propose is not only tricky, but also risky (he said sarcastically).

ASK them! In other words, use the 20-Foot Rule. It's really just that simple.

Interestingly, many leaders won't ask what's de-motivating their team members because either:

1. They make the assumption that they already know (their assumptions are often incorrect, by the way)
2. They honestly don't even think to ask (well intended, but in the dark)
3. They perceive themselves to be too busy to ask (other things are perceived to be more important)
4. They don't really want to know (especially if they think they may be part of the problem)
5. They really already do know, but are unwilling to make the changes necessary to turn the situation around (stubborn)
6. They really already do know, but don't know how to go about changing it (skill-deficit)
7. They think this is just a temporary situation that will resolve itself on its own (wishful thinkers)
8. They simply don't care (The beatings will continue until morale improves!)

Did you know that **not** asking about, identifying, and then moving to remove the de-motivators from your environment can, in and of itself, be one of the **principle** de-motivators in your environment?

In other words, you can take a major step toward purging the de-motivating factors in your environment simply by genuinely asking people what they are.

Here's another way this point has been illustrated to me:

Many of my corporate clients conduct employee opinion surveys and often the most common areas of concern that surface in many of these survey results boil down to 2 very interesting things:

1. There is a perceived lack of recognition for a job well done
2. Not enough is being done about people who aren't doing their jobs and/or poor performers

Note: You may recall these issues from the chapter on Leadership Reality Checks.

Both of those factors can be *huge* de-motivators!

So, if you're interested in re-establishing a "motivated" work/team environment, you might want to start by making sure you tackle these 2 big de-motivators that may well be lurking in your midst. My belief is that:

1. If you do this with genuineness of heart, while
2. Actively seeking out information on what other de-motivators may exist, and
3. Then act decisively to remove or at least marginalize the de-motivating factors in your organization

You'll find that a "motivated" environment will begin to re-establish itself where you work and/or play.

Do I really believe this? I do indeed! And remember, this is coming from someone who's often billed/presented to others as a "Motivational Speaker".

Here's a little secret: I'm not really even very fond of the title *"Motivational Speaker"*. That's why you won't find those 2 words in combination anywhere in this book or on my website except where you just read them in this sentence!

It's my belief that if you give people a positive vision of what and who they can become, help them remove the obstacles (including a lack of information) from their path, and give them the practical tools critical to their successful journey, you can rest assured *they'll* provide all the fuel necessary for their *own* motivation.

When employees provide their own fuel for motivation, the likelihood that your organization will operate at a consistently high level is significantly increased.

I'm just sayin'.

CHAPTER 12

THE PHYSICS OF SUSTAINED OPERATIONAL EXCELLENCE

One of the keys to sustaining operational excellence is to understand a couple of laws of physics – namely the difference between *momentum* and *impetus*, and how each can impact your organization. Both of these terms deal with the physics of motion. They are often used interchangeably. In reality however, while they are similar, when you drill down a bit you will find them to be quite different. For the sake of definition let's take a look in a scientific sense at what each of these terms mean.

Let's begin with a simple example.

Let's say there is a car that is rolling down hill. As long as it is on a downward slope and the brakes aren't engaged, the car will continue to move forward and will even begin to gain speed, even if the accelerator pedal isn't pressed.

As the car reaches an even or level grade, unless the accelerator pedal is pressed, it will begin to slow its forward progress and will eventually come to a stop.

If the same car reaches an uphill grade before it stops rolling, it will slow more quickly, and unless the brakes are applied, the car will begin to roll backward.

If the accelerator pedal is not pushed while the car is on the uphill grade, it will never progress further on the upward slope beyond where the brakes were applied.

This scenario mirrors the struggle that many organizations face, but more on that later. Let's get to the laws of physics present in this scenario.

As the car is moving down hill, the law of physics that is in play is *Impetus.*

Impetus is a force that compels an object to move. As the car moves downhill, it is actually gravity that is compelling its forward motion. In other words, absent the pressing of the accelerator pedal, gravity is providing the impetus for the cars' motion.

As the car reaches a level grade it continues to move forward. The law of physics in play here is ***momentum***. Momentum is the product of the mass and velocity of an object. In more practical terms, momentum is the motion experienced by an object *after* it receives some push or compelling force.

If the car continues on an even or level grade, without some impetus (i. e. the accelerator being pressed), it will eventually come to a stop.

Therein lies the problem with too much of a reliance on momentum. Momentum, in and of its self, is not self-sustaining. An object (or organization) that relies too heavily on momentum will tend to ebb and flow based on the terrain it encounters.

Organizations that have periods of operational excellence separated by periods of "acceptable" or sometimes even mediocre performance tend to be those that rely too much upon momentum. This level of consistency tends to be anything but, as they tend to have dramatic swings in their level of operational effectiveness. Translation – They do well when rolling downhill but struggle when they encounter the upward slopes of adversity.

The most successful organizations, however, tend to operate with an impetus mindset. They tend not to rely on momentum or even the situational or naturally occurring impetus that is supplied by the terrain they must navigate.

They understand, for example, that the same impetus (gravity) that can move you forward can also pull you backward, if you encounter an upward slope (difficult economic conditions, increased competition, etc.).

Instead, the most successful of organizations focus on creating their own impetus. They understand that to keep the object (organization) moving forward in a consistent manner, they must compel it to do so. Simply put, they focus on keeping their foot on the accelerator.

In successful organizations, impetus is supplied by constantly ensuring that:

- Organizational Goals and Priorities "Big Rocks" are clear and well communicated

- Expectations for team members are crystal clear and those expectations are clearly linked to the organization's "Big Rocks"
- Training and instruction is used to address *skill* deficits (not *will* deficits)
- Team members are regularly engaged in problem solving and solution implementing activities
- Metrics and Data are being used wisely
- Meaningful recognition is an integral part of the organizational equation
- Accountability is firmly entrenched in the culture of the organization
- Team members always have an idea where they stand with performance because of the consistent use of efficient and effective feedback
- Effective communication is the norm
- Future leaders are in the "pipeline" and are being prepared to take the helm before they have that responsibility

Operating with an impetus mentality vs. a momentum dependent mentality keeps the organization focused through times of adversity. Indeed, an impetus mentality creates an atmosphere whereas the people in the organization proactively plan for the uphill slopes and strategize in advance about ways to keep their foot on the accelerator.

In a nutshell, to give your organization the best possible chance to sustain operational excellence, focus on the compelling forces necessary to drive the organization forward (impetus) and not just on what happens after you apply the compelling force (momentum).

"Getting There and Staying There" when it comes to sustaining operational excellence is all about Impetus.

Thus ends this physics lesson.

Thus ends this book.

ABOUT THE AUTHOR

Greg Gray is the Founder and President of Renaissance Unlimited, Inc. - a professional and personal leadership firm based in Atlanta, Georgia, and is one of the most sought after speakers on the speaking and seminar circuit today.

His keynotes, seminars and workshops have electrified and empowered tens of thousands of people in more than 400 hundred cities all across America, the Caribbean, Europe, and the Pacific Rim. Greg's blend of humor and real world, practical ideas on leadership, service, and relationship building are receiving rave reviews from clients that run the gamut of Industries and Associations all over the country.

In 1994, Greg co-authored the largest Customer Service training course in United States history. This program, entitled "Excellent Service! Handle with Care!", was attended by more than 110,000 U. S. Postal Service employees and has become a standard video training series for all new USPS Retail employees.

More recently, Greg has developed the "Renaissance Series" - a number of seminars, training, and keynote topics designed to deal with a variety of issues around the subjects of leadership, communication, relationship building, and enhancing the external and internal customer experience. A number of these programs are also available on DVD.

Greg received his bachelor's degree in Communications from Oberlin College, and has more than 30 years of experience working in Sales, Customers Service, Training, and Management in industries ranging from Retail to Telecommunications.

Greg's success can be attributed to his consistent themes of personal responsibility and profit through service!

For more information...
On Greg's programs on DVD, books, or to book him for a seminar or speaking opportunity for your organization call us at **770-498-9755**, email us at **greg@greggray. com** or visit Greg's website at **greggray. com.**

Join Greg on Facebook @ Facebook. com/greggrayonfb
Follow Greg on Twitter @greggray925

Also from Greg Gray

Dad from a Distance
How non-custodial Fathers can still be fantastic Dads
Available now at greggray.com, amazon.com, and on Kindle.

Upcoming Books from Greg Gray

Wake Me When it's Over!
Why so many presentations suck and yours don't have to

If *BEFORE* All Else Fails
Things to consider before you run out of things to consider

Families on the Blend
How to keep your Family Merger from feeling like a Hostile Take-over

17756635R10128

Made in the USA
Charleston, SC
27 February 2013